PRISONER FOR PEACE:

Aung San Suu Kyi

AND

Burma's Struggle For Democracy

PRISONER

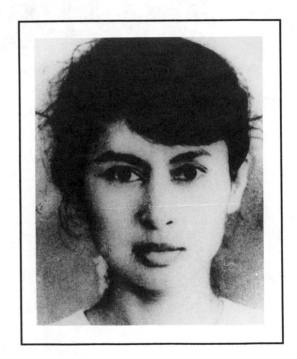

—————————————— Champions of Freedom

FOR PEACE:

Aung San Suu Kyi

AND

Burma's Struggle For Democracy

JOHN PARENTEAU

Morgan Reynolds Inc.
Greensboro

PRISONER FOR PEACE:

Aung San Suu Kyi

AND

Burma's Struggle For Democracy

Library of Congress Cataloging-in-Publication Data
Parenteau, John, 1957-
    Prisoner for peace: Aung San Suu Kyi and Burma's struggle for democracy / John
Parenteau.
        p. cm. -- (Champions of freedom)
    Includes bibliographical references and index.
    ISBN   1-883846-05-6
    1. Aung San Suu Kyi.. 2. Burma--Politics and government--1948-
3. Politicians--Burma--Biography.   I. Series: Champions of freedom.
(Greensboro, NC)
DS530. 53. A85P37   1994
959. 105' 092--dc20
[B}
                                                           94-4100
                                                            CIP

Printed in the United States of America

First Edition

5 4 3 2 1

**Dedicated
to
Michelle and Matthew**

CONTENTS

ACKNOWLEDGEMENTS

The historical information for Burma is based on three sources: John F. Cady's *A History of Modern Burma*, Frank N. Trager's *Burma: From Kingdom to Republic: A Historical and Political Analysis*, and Maung Htin Aung's *A History of Burma*.

Biographical information about Aung San Suu Kyi has been assembled from *Freedom From Fear*, the collection of Aung San Suu Kyi's writings, articles her husband Michael Aris has published, and information in *Current Biography* and the *New York Times Biographical Service*.

Bertil Lintner in *The Far Eastern Economic Review*, Steven Erlanger in *The New York Times*, and the *Times* of London have reported extensively on recent events in Burma. Lintner has collected his reporting into a book, *Outrage: Burma's Struggle for Democracy*, and a pamphlet, *Aung San Suu Kyi and The Unfinished Burmese Reanissance*. Mya Maung, a Burmese economist now living in the United States, based *Totalitarianism in Burma* on interviews with eyewitnesses to the events.

I must thank my wife for allowing me the time to write, the library staffs who helped with the research, and Mr. David Piatt for his steadfast encouragement.

A NOTE ON NAMES

The Burmese traditionally use five titles with their names: *U, Maung, Daw, Ma,* and *Ko.*

U (pronounced like the "oo" in "zoo") literaly means "Uncle," but equates to the English term "Mister." *Maung* and *Ko* ("elder brother" and "younger brother") are equivalent to English's "Master." *Daw* ("Aunt") equates to "Mrs." *Ma* ("sister") is equivalent to "Miss." In Burma, however, these terms relate more closely to social standing than to marital status. Upon marriage, women are given the title *Daw,* but adult women of respectable standing who are not married are also addressed as *Daw.*

Names are further complicated because U and Maung are also commonly used as names. *U* (Uncle) Tin U and *Maung* (Brother) Maung Gyi, both characters you will encounter in this book, are examples. Titles will be printed in italics, while names will appear in regular type.

Burmese parents do not attach a family name, or surname, to their children's name. Because women do not take their husband's name upon marriage, it is possible, even common, for a Burmese family to have father, mother, sons and daughters with entirely different names. However, there has recently been a trend to include the parent's name in the children's. For example, *U* Aung San and *Daw* Khin Kyi named their sons Aung San U and Aung San Lin, and their daughter Aung San Suu Kyi.

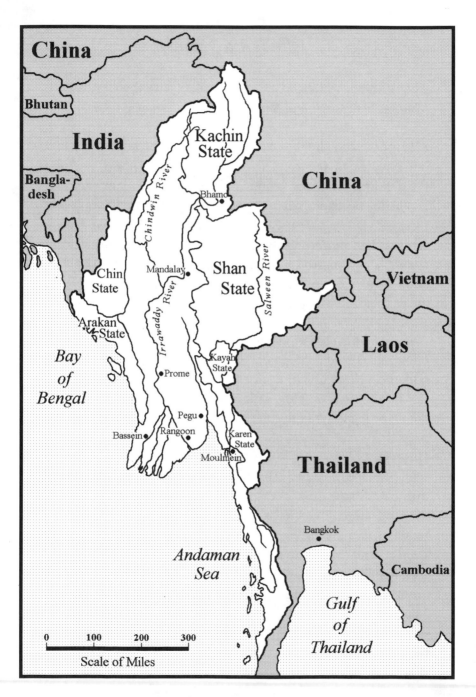

Map Of Burma (Myanmar)

ONE

THE GUEST OF HONOR
CAN'T BE HERE

On December 10, 1991, over 1500 dignitaries from around the world gathered at City Hall in Oslo, Norway, to attend the presentation of the 1991 Nobel Peace Prize. Several former Peace Prize winners were in the hall to commemorate the ninetieth anniversary of the Prize.

Daw (Mrs.) Aung San Suu Kyi, a Burmese political dissident, won the Peace Prize that year. Michael Aris, Suu's British husband, was there. Suu and Michael's two teenaged sons, Alexander and Kim, were there. But Aung San Suu Kyi was not. She was imprisoned in her house in Rangoon, Burma, where military authorities had held her in isolation since July 1989.

Alexander and Kim accepted the award for their mother. When Professor Francis Sejerstedt, the Chairman of the Nobel Committee, delivered the gold medallion to Alexander and the honorary diploma to Kim, the auditorium responded with a standing ovation.

Then, standing before the crowd, sixteen-year-old Alexander Aris spoke for his mother. Suu, Alexander said, "would say this prize belongs not to her but to all those men, women and children who, even as I speak, continue to sacrifice their well being, their freedom and their lives in pursuit of a democratic Burma."[1] Then his voice filled with emotion. "Speaking as her son," Alexander continued, "I would add that I personally believe that by her own dedication and personal sacrifice she has come to be a worthy symbol through whom the plight of all the people of Burma may be recognized."[2]

That evening, in the bitter cold of a long Scandinavian night, Gro Harlem Brundtland, the Prime Minister of Norway, led hundreds of Burmese dissidents in a candlelight march through the streets of Oslo. In Burma, university students marked the award ceremony with protests against the government. At least two of the students were reported killed that day. Perhaps as many as 900 were arrested. *Daw Aung San Suu Kyi*, the symbol of so much protest, sat alone and imprisoned in her house on University Avenue in Rangoon, surrounded by troops.

Burma, officially known in the United Nations as Myanmar since June 1989, is a country rich in resources but poor in political stability. A British colony in the nineteenth and early twentieth centuries, Burma won its independence from Great Britain after World War II. Since then, it has suffered almost constant internal strife. A democratic state at independence, it has been ruled by military and socialist dictatorships since 1962.

Many people know Burma only as a peaceful and placid land of golden pagodas and friendly, smiling people. But periods of unrest have shaken this beautiful country several times since the military took control. The latest, begun in 1988, brought forth promises from the government of "free and fair" democratic elections. The government, confident that no one could unite the country against them, felt they could most easily pacify the populace by allowing elections. After 26 years of political monopoly, Burma's rulers believed they could emerge from even a reasonably honest election as the one party that could dominate a new government.

But they had overlooked *Daw* Aung San Suu Kyi. The daughter of *U* (Mr.) Aung San, Burma's most revered hero of World War II and the fight for independence, Suu returned to Burma from her home in Oxford, England, in 1988 to nurse her ill mother. When the government promised to hold elections, Suu was drawn into the opposition movement. With nothing more than her firm belief in peace and democracy, and her father's name for a banner, she united a badly divided opposition, in which over two hundred political parties registered to participate in the election.

The government realized its mistake too late. By July 1989, they knew the opposition would unite behind Aung San Suu Kyi's National League for Democracy (NLD), and the military rulers would be shut out from the new government. International opinion forbade cancellation of the elections, so the opposition had to be divided to ensure the ruling party would retain the dominant voice in Burma's government. Suu and most of her fellow opposition leaders were arrested.

Confident again, the government permitted elections to be held in May 1990. The result stunned Burma and the world: Suu's National League for Democracy won in a landslide, despite the fact that most of its top leaders were being held in prison. Forced either to concede defeat or to crack down on the populace, the military government chose the latter.

After the election, unrest continued. The government, which had used every tactic to win the election from scurrilous cartoons to mass killings, tightened its grip again. Five years and many thousands of deaths later, Burma has still not settled down. One major unifying force which has kept the unrest alive is *Daw* Aung San Suu Kyi. This is her story. But it is Burma's story as well.

TWO

THE KINGDOM OF BURMA

A college friend of Aung San Suu Kyi once described her as so typically "Burmese" that even thirty years of living abroad could not hide her Burmese upbringing. But what is this vague "Burmeseness" that can't be hidden? To understand Suu, we must first understand Burma.

The Land and People

About the size and population of California and Arizona combined, Burma is located along the eastern shore of the Bay of Bengal in southeast Asia. Bordered on the west by Bangladesh and India, on the north by China, and on the east by Laos and Thailand, Burma has a history strongly tied to those countries. Roughly diamond-shaped, the country is aptly described as a kite with a tail.

Burma is a land of great variations. The landscape changes dramatically from coastal plains that are drenched by torrential monsoon-season rains almost six months each year, to a hot, dry central plateau, to high, sometimes cold mountain jungles along the borders. Burma has three well defined seasons: the rainy season from May to October, the cool season from November to February, and the hot season from March to May.

Burma is rich in natural resources. For thousands of years travellers have known the country as a "Land of Gold." Its hills hold some of the world's finest teak forests as well as large deposits of minerals and gemstones, especially rubies and jade. Considerable oil fields have been tapped in the twentieth century. Large stretches of irrigated rice fields along the coast and the delta of the Irrawaddy river, Burma's longest, once provided one-third of the world's supply of rice, as well as many other crops from cotton to sugar cane. In recent years, as the economy has deteriorated, poppy production, from which opium and heroin are extracted, has become a main source of income in the hills.

Burma never has been a strongly united country. Over one hundred ethnic groups, with ties throughout southern and central Asia, make up the population. The three main groups are the "Tibeto-Burmans", the Mons, and the Shans. Most of the "Tibeto-Burmans" are called Burmans, Suu's ethnic group. The Burmans account for about two-thirds of Burma's approximately forty million people. Other large "Tibeto-Burman" groups closely related to the Burmans are the Chins and Kachins, who live in the mountains along the border with India and China, the Arakans, who live on the coast north of the Irrawaddy River delta, and the Karens, who live in the southern hills and river valleys.

The Mons live in Burma's southern tail, and are more closely related to the Khmer people of Cambodia than to the Burmans.

The third major ethnic group is the Shans, who are related to the people of Laos and Thailand. The Shans live on the eastern part of Burma's central plateau and in the mountains along the Thai border.

The Mons, Arakans, Karens, Shans, and Chins all have distinct, well-developed cultures and a history of periodic independence from the Burmans.

Burma also has a large immigrant population. Indians, both Hindu and Muslim, have come to Burma for many centuries. Chinese frequently have emigrated from the north. Many westerners, mainly British and British-Indians, have lived in Burma since the early years of European exploration. American Baptist missionaries arrived on the Tenasserim coast in 1813.

More than ancestry divides the people of Burma. Most

ethnic groups speak separate languages, though Burmese has become the national language and English is widely known.

Before the British built railroads, geography isolated the many peoples of Burma. Rivers draining the central plateau, especially the Irrawaddy, were the main highways. But in the hills, the rivers were too small to navigate. During the monsoons from May to October, many land roads became impassable muck. As a result, the people along the borders lived isolated from the Burmans on the central plateau. Even today, travel can be difficult during some parts of the year.

Most Burmese are Buddhists. Buddhism originated in northern India between 600 and 500 B.C., when Siddhartha Gautama, a wealthy Indian prince, turned away from his worldly wealth to seek spiritual knowledge. Buddhists believe that by acquiring wisdom and love—good will to all—one can overcome the pain and evil of the world and attain the perfect state, *nirvana*. Siddhartha was the most influential of the Buddhas (enlightened ones) who have walked the earth teaching the way to *nirvana*.

Over the next thousand years, Indian evangelists spread Buddhism throughout southeast Asia. The Burmans, historians believe, received Buddhism from two Indian missionaries who arrived between 250 and 200 BC. The Mons adopted Theravada Buddhism very early. After King

Anawrahta conquered the Mons of southern Burma 12 centuries later in 1044, Theravada Buddhism became the dominant form of Buddhism in all of Burma. Theravada (Way of the Elders), a form of Buddhism common throughout southeast Asia, stresses active benevolence—doing good deeds—toward every living thing. This tradition, which among Christians might be expressed as "do unto others as you would have others do unto you," is intended to lead Theravada Buddhists to treat people of different classes, races, and religions charitably. Burmese Buddhists do not follow a rigid class, or Caste distinction, as do most Hindus. Theravada Buddhists also consider women the equals of men. For a Buddhist, it is difficult to have true "good will" for someone you treat as your inferior. Buddhism is a religion which overcomes worldly problems not by conquering them, but by understanding them and learning to make the best of them. Unlike westerners, who always must be "going" and "doing", Buddhists tend to be contemplative. One historian, John F. Cady, aptly called Buddhism "a religion of withdrawal" from worldly problems.[3]

Though a large majority of the population practices Theravada Buddhism, Burmese religions also vary widely. Many of the ethnic groups retain a spirit-worship which predates Buddhism. In fact, even many Buddhists still pay tribute to a group of 37 spirits known as "*Nats*," which have no relation to the Buddhist faith. The Karens are animists. They believe that everything, living or not, has a soul. A traditional Karen legend tells of a white traveller from the sea who would return their "lost book" to them. When American Baptist missionaries arrived on the coast of Burma carrying bibles in 1813, they seemed to fulfill the legend so closely that Karens were relatively easy to convert. As a result, the Karens have the strongest Christian community among all the Burmese. In the twentieth century, many Kachins in the northeast and Nagas along the Indian border have adopted Christianity.

The Kingdom of Burma

The various Burmese people were united under one king three times during the 800 years before the British arrived in Burma.

The "First Unification" of Burma began in 1044, when the Burman King Anawrahta began conquering the surrounding areas. Anawrahta's military exploits quickly became legendary. Chronicles survive which tell of Anawrahta and his four generals, clad in golden armor, charging into battle atop demon-like horses. Anawrahta was a military innovator. He was among the first warriors to use elephants like tanks, thundering ahead of his soldiers to put fear into the hearts of his foes. Even Anawrahta's own men must have feared him. The slightest disobedience brought one punishment: Death! Anawrahta died in 1077, but the dynasty he founded lasted until 1287, when Mongols invading from China sacked the city of Pagan, Anawrahta's capital. The Shans in eastern Burma and the coastal Arakans and Mons then shook off Burman rule.

Burma remained fractured for two centuries. Then, between 1486 and 1531, Burman King Minkyinyo conquered the surrounding areas, reuniting Burma in what is known as the "Second Unification," which lasted just over 200 years. In 1729, the Mons rebelled against the Burmans. At first the war went well for the Mons, but after capturing the Burman capital at Ava, they ran out of luck. The Mons were defeated about 1755, and their capital city of Pegu was destroyed. With the defeat of the Mons, Burma's "tail" was reattached, and the "Third Unification" of Burma began.

Though the kings' power grew and shrank, the Burmese Kingdom remained basically unchanged from Anawrahta's reign until the British conquest in 1885. The reigning king rarely enjoyed control over all his lands. Many groups, especially the Shans in the east, ruled themselves to a large degree, paying nominal tribute to the Burman king.

But where the king did rule, his authority was absolute. Before the British arrived, Burma had no constitution defining the government: the king was the government. *Min*, the Burmese word for "king," is also the word for "government". The king appointed all government officials down to the village level. *Myothugyis*, village officials whose responsibilities were comparable to those of a Justice of the Peace, had some hereditary right to office that remained from the time before the First Unification. Only below the *myothugyi*, about the level of village tax assessor, did the Burmese people have some choice in who their leaders were.

The King made all laws and the *Hluttaw*, his royal council, executed them. There was no legislature to construct a legal code, nor was there a court system to review the laws. Because all power resided in the king, little protected the Burmese people from a cruel monarch. Stories of atrocities committed by kings pepper Burmese history books. Many kings executed rivals for the throne. King Anawrahta, like Herod in ancient Israel, is said to have killed children and even pregnant women to protect his throne. While tales such as King Anawrahta's are more legend than historical fact, clearly the abuse of power was widespread. The king's advisors, for their own safety, were frequently little more than "yes" men. In a world where losing one's position at court and losing one's head often went hand in hand, disagreement was dangerous.

Buddhism was one check on the king's authority. The protection and advancement of Buddhism ranked high among the king's duties. Though not the official head of a church, as the Pope is head of the Roman Catholic Church, the Burmese king was the mentor of the Buddhist clergy, or *sangha*. Over many years Buddhism had developed a series of "laws, precepts, and rules" governing the actions of a good king. A good king would respect Buddhism, protect and give alms (charitable donations) to the *sangha*, and honor the *Nats*. He would be gentle and generous, control his anger, and not mistreat his subjects. He would heed the people's will and the wise council of his advisors. These rules were not laws which could be used to depose a unpopular king, but only guidelines. If a king followed the "laws, precepts, and rules," it was believed that prosperity would follow: if he violated them, ruin.

Sometimes monks intervened to save the life of someone who had aroused the king's anger. In fact, one common way to rescue a condemned man from the king was to ordain him a monk. Even a king had great respect for the *sangha*. Frequently he spared the life of a newly ordained monk rather than offend the clergy.

The only other control on a king was rebellion. When a king's actions became too harsh to tolerate, it was easier— and sometimes safer—to revolt against him than to advise him to change his ways. Even after years of contact with westerners, Burmese kings had little understanding of the concept of a parliamentary system with a "loyal opposition." In the 1870's, for example, King Mindon and British Prime Minister William Gladstone attempted to resolve the confrontations which would eventually lead to the final British conquest of Burma in 1885. Mindon even became fond of Gladstone. When Benjamin Disraeli succeeded Gladstone as British Prime Minister, Mindon was saddened. "Poor Gladstone," Mindon said. "I am sorry for him. I don't think he was a bad fellow. . . ." Mindon assumed his friend was in prison, or dead.[4]

Mindon could well assume this. The transfer of the Burmese crown from his brother King Pagan to himself had taken place in classic Burmese style: by revolution. A den of gambling and vice, Pagan's court had a well-deserved reputation for moral laxness. After the frivolous Pagan lost the second British-Burmese war in 1852, his brother Mindon emerged from a Buddhist monastery, where he had been a monk, to seize the throne. Ex-King Pagan survived the transfer of power, but only because Mindon was a wise and compassionate ruler. (Mindon was the only king of the Third

Unification who did not execute the king he replaced.)

Luckily for the people, Burmese kings had little to do in a country where subsistence farming ruled the economy. Beyond raising armies, the kings usually left the people to themselves. Though their absolute power sometimes led them to abuse the people, the kings of Burma are best described as benign, if not benevolent. They did little good, but caused little harm. People asked no favors of the government and expected nothing in return except taxes, military conscription, and occasional minor abuse.

Life in Burma Today

What can be said about life in Burma now? It is risky to describe a "typical" person, but we can try to describe how life in Burma appears to an outsider.

Many rural Burmese families live much as their ancestors did. They are Buddhists. They visit the nearby pagodas regularly to pray and to meditate, and are generous with the monks who come begging alms.

They live in a village, close to their relatives, and make their livings as farmers. They are more or less self sufficient, and so ask little of their government and take little notice of it. They may still pay taxes with a portion of their crop.

The wife probably defers to the husband in family matters, but sees herself as his equal. "We Burmese women like *to let* our men be head of the house," says one Burmese woman. A Burmese wife owns her own property, and can easily divorce her husband. In fact, women have long enjoyed equality with men. Historical records attest to women serving as public officials since before Anawrahta's time. Several British writers of a century ago declared that the typical nineteenth-century Burmese woman had better rights than any woman in Europe. In many families, the wife will conduct the business side of farming, buying the supplies and selling the crops.

Even before the British arrived, most Burmese probably were literate. Historically, Burmese boys have been educated in the local monastery, and girls in the home. The girls are strongly disciplined by their mothers, but the boys are allowed to run free. At about age eight, however, they will go to the monastery, as did their fathers, to study for a year or two. Under the monks' stern care they will learn Buddhism, reading and writing, and also discipline and respect for their elders. A few will take the oaths of a Buddhist novitiate and go on to become full-fledged monks, but most will return to the worldly lives their studies interrupted. They return not as unruly boys, but as disciplined young men, ready to shoulder their part of the family burden.

The rural family's life revolves around the seasons, and work is sporadic but hard. The rice planting and harvesting seasons are back-breaking toil for all. Slack times after the rice harvest are often filled with *pwes*, celebrations given for almost any occasion. The birth of a child, a house-raising, a business success, a death, a wedding—even a divorce, is justification for hosting a *pwe*. Shway Yoe, an English writer who grew to like the Burmese so well he used a Burmese pseudonym, wrote, half jokingly, "whenever in fact anything at all is done," there is a *pwe*. Most people define *"pwe"* to mean "play," but *pwes* are much more than dramatic performances. *Pwes* involve the entire community, either participating or watching, and often continue all day. It is a rare Burmese who has not acted in a local *pwe*.

For a break during a hard day, a Burmese might spend an afternoon playing *gonnyinto*, a game similar to pitching pennies. *Gonnyinto* tempts one to bet recklessly, leading to frequent brawls and occasional murder. Another popular game is *chinlon*, which Americans call hacky-sac. Played with a woven wicker ball, *chinlon* can amuse a Burmese child for hours.

A modern, urban Burmese family retains many features from their ancestors and rural countrymen. They remain devout Buddhists. Though education is no longer centered in the monasteries, many young boys are still sent to study with the monks. (Both of Suu's sons, though they had lived their entire lives outside Burma, were taken there by their parents to take their monk's vows when they came of age.) They are friendly, neighborly, and concerned about their fellows' welfare.

Modern Burmese, like their predecessors, still have a lingering belief in *Nats*, and may choose to do things at astrologically favorable dates and times. One of the largest—and bloodiest—demonstrations in Rangoon began at the auspicious time of 8:08 in the morning on August 8, 1988: 8-8-88.

Many modern Burmese still strongly respect authority. One Burmese scholar has said the Burmese will tolerate anything from their government except mass starvation. Americans, who consider the freedom to criticize their government a birthright, might say the Burmese are respectful to a fault. They show a level of respect for their elders which is difficult for many youth-oriented westerners to understand.

Two traits that have emerged repeatedly in Burmese politics are intense loyalty and sensitivity to criticism. These tendencies can make Burmese politics extremely personal and volatile. As the historian David I. Steinberg put it, "Power has always been intensely personal in Burma; loyalty within the government is to the person, not the institution."[5] Political leaders have tended to take criticism personally, and to react to it violently.

Burma is a highly complicated country, with many ancient traditions that have survived into the modern world. However, present day Burma is not only the product of internal development. For many years Burma was a colony dominated by Europeans, especially the British. To understand the history of Burma, and its present day political turmoil, we need to look at how colonialism influenced the development of Burmese society and politics.

THREE

COLONIAL BURMA

When the Burmese first met westerners in the sixteenth century, Spain and Portugal ruled the waves. In 1494, those two countries had arrogantly divided the globe between themselves. Burma fell into the Portuguese half. When they arrived, the Portuguese found Burma newly reunited under King Minkyinyo. In addition to a healthy trade in precious metals, gems, exotic Pegu pottery, and teak, many Portuguese sailors found employment as mercenaries in Burma's army.

Within one hundred years, British, French, and Dutch merchants had all formed trading companies of their own to compete from Africa to Taiwan. From 1600 to about 1760, the British East India Company gradually took over all of India. French trade centered in what is now Thailand, Cambodia, and Vietnam. Sandwiched between British India and French-dominated Indo-China, the Kingdom of

Burma jealously guarded its independence and welcomed a careful, evenhanded trade with all the Europeans.

When the Mons in Tenassarim, the southeast "tail" of Burma, revolted against Burman rule in 1729, they expelled the British, who had built shipyards along the coast, and sought aid from the French. After suppressing the rebellion, Burman King Alaungpaya met with Robert Lester, a representative of the British East India Company. They signed a treaty of friendship on July 28, 1757, the first formal agreement between Burma and the West. The pact gave the British East India Company exclusive rights to trade with the Burmese, in exchange for guns and a military alliance. Despite this agreement, the Burmese continued to trade with the French and other Europeans in the region.

Though British India and Burma argued over their border, it was the pursuit of money—the basic reason the British were in southeast Asia in the first place—that finally brought the British into conflict with Burma. After discovering that they could "buy goods for 3,000 pounds sterling in Calcutta, and sell them for 8,000 in Burma,"[6] a short sail across the Bay of Bengal, the British naturally wanted to begin trading. France was proving also that a lucrative trade with the interior of China existed, if only the traders could get there. To British merchants, Burma's Irrawaddy River looked like a smooth highway for flowing goods into China and taking money out.

Between 1795 and 1824, Britain sent many emissaries to Burma, seeking pacification of the border, exclusion of their French competition, and ever-increasing trade opportunities.

Behind the scene, Indian Governor-general Richard Wellesley, who wanted British control extended over all southeast Asia, waited for an opportunity to take Burma by force. Border disputes provided plenty of excuse, but not until 1824, long after Wellesley had left India, could an assault be launched on Burma. The British-Burmese war of 1824 ended quickly, leaving Britain in control of Arakan, the rice-rich part of the Burmese coastline bordering India, and Tenassarim, which had desirable seaports and access to forests of teak, a wood highly prized in Europe.

Immediately, the British Governor-general replaced the king's officials and hereditary village *myothugyis* with a bureaucracy designed like the British administration in India. The Indian system had evolved over a century and a half, giving Indians time to adjust and learn to respect the new order. The Burmese, however, fell under British control in just a few months. The new British system of legislatures and impersonal and procedure-bound courts, which both punished the guilty and protected the innocent, was too foreign to command instantaneous respect. Many Englishmen thought they were "freeing" the Burmese people from a despotic king, but, as the historian John F. Cady put it, "Far from resenting the necessity of grovelling before a king, as westerners assumed that the Burmese should do, the people recognized. . . that a king was a sorely needed symbol of authority."[7] And a Christian king in England would not do as a "symbol of authority" in Buddhist Burma. Many Burmese turned to lawlessness.

Perhaps more importantly, the war revolutionized the economy of conquered "lower" Burma. The new economy was run for the benefit of British and Indian business interests. Though the British invested an enormous amount of money in Burma, it brought little direct good but much harm to the people for many years. Much of the money never circulated in Burma. Indian workers sent as much as 90% of their wages to their families in India, and British workers, many of whom considered their stays in Burma temporary get-rich-quick situations, banked theirs in England. So Burmese merchants and shopkeepers never saw a piece of the economic pie.

Before the British arrived, rice had been the foundation of Burma's economy. Rice was so important that its export was strictly regulated by the king, and laws guaranteed each farmer's right to food despite his debts, protecting him against starvation in years when the harvest was poor. But to the British, rice was just another thing to sell. They exported rice in enormous amounts, but the profit from those sales went to British merchants and Indian money-lenders, not to the Burmese. Worse, they held back no reserve. Now, in years when the harvest failed, the Burmese faced starvation. As rice production skyrocketed in re-sponse to increased exports, more and more land was needed. People began burning jungle to provide new land to plant with rice. Clearing new land cost money. This meant mortgages, something new for the Burmese. Most farmers eventually lost their land, becoming instead low-paid mi-grant workers. Traditional Burmese ties to the land began dying out. Along with a monetary system came wage labor and periodic unemployment during the long months be-tween rice planting and harvesting. Almost overnight, a western-style consumer economy overran the sleepy Bur-mese subsistence farmers.

The British brought some real advantages, but they rarely came without a cost. New ideas of individualism were balanced by a decreasing respect for the Buddhist *sangha*. Easier travel and movement allowed by the new railroads had to be balanced against the increased lawlessness result-ing from the loss of family ties and traditional authority figures. It was not until almost 1900 that Burmese society again settled down.

If the 1824 war had some justification in the border dispute, the 1852 war between British India and Burma was clearly instigated to add to Britain's colonial possessions. British naval officers, angry over fines the Burmese imposed for violations of harbor rules, demanded the Burmese repay the fines—ten times over—and apologize. When the Burmese refused, Lord James Dalhousie, the British Governor-general in India, demanded, on pain of war, payment of a huge ransom and an official apology from the king. Basically, Britain held Burma hostage. The Burmese, naturally, refused. War was inevitable.

British forces advanced up the Irrawaddy River, taking large tracts of prime rice land, and moved toward the Burmese capital at Ava. The war quickly came to an end when Mindon overthrew his brother, King Pagan, and accepted without question the existing British lines. British India now controlled the entire Burmese coastline and much of Burma's most productive agricultural land. Though no peace treaty was ever signed, Mindon did sign a commercial treaty in 1862, ten years after the war's end.

Governor-General Dalhousie argued that Burmese stubbornness had thrust the war upon him, but even at that time many British saw through the shallow excuse for the war. "Nobody gives us credit for sincerity," Richard Cobden, an Englishman argued, "when we protest our reluctance to acquire more territory, whilst our actions are thus falsifying all our professions. Ought not we to advertize in the *Times*, for a Governor-General of India who can collect a debt of a thousand pounds without annexing a territory?"[8]

Yet some British thought the war had ended too soon. They said all of Burma should have been taken, and the Burmese king reduced to a British vassal, as had been India's princes. Britain both wanted and needed Burma. As John F. Cady said, "Burma was caught firmly in the squeeze between rival European imperialisms."[9] The French had finally figured out how to reach China's Yunnan province— along Vietnam's Red River instead of Cambodia's Mekong. Britain desperately needed access to the Irrawaddy River route if it wanted to compete with France for China's desirable silk, velvet, gold-leaf, and tea trade.

The chance came soon. Mindon died in 1878. His son and successor, Thibaw, was a weak and brutal leader. Against Mindon's deathbed wish, Thibaw seized the throne. To strengthen his rule, he married one of his half-sisters and put to death his other brothers, sisters, and cousins—anyone who could challenge him.

Using Thibaw's brutality to gain public support, the British again seized on money as a cause for war. Thibaw imposed a huge fine on the Burma-Bombay Trading Company for illegally cutting teak trees in the forests of Thibaw's kingdom. The fine, though large, was allowed under the treaty Mindon had signed in 1862. In response, the British agreed to talk about paying some smaller fine, provided the Burmese granted British traders access to the China trade routes.

Cut off from the sea by British Burma, and from China by a rebellion in China's Yunnan province, Thibaw's remnant Kingdom of Burma greatly needed British trade. Still, Thibaw thought he could get it on his own terms, and declared that the fines were non-negotiable; trade access would be granted only after the fine was paid. This the British dismissed as an "unconditional refusal." Again, war was on.

Within two weeks, the British-Indian forces overran the Burmese capital, which Thibaw had moved to Mandalay. On November 28, 1885, Thibaw surrendered to the British. Burma became a British colony, and the Burmese Kingdom was a part of history. Thibaw, denied even a symbolic throne like those granted India's princes, went into exile near Bombay, India, where he died in 1916.

From the start, the British had looked down on the Burmese. As *Maung* Htin Aung, a Burmese historian, put it, "A long line of British officials. . . had the greatest contempt for the Burmese, closing their eyes deliberately

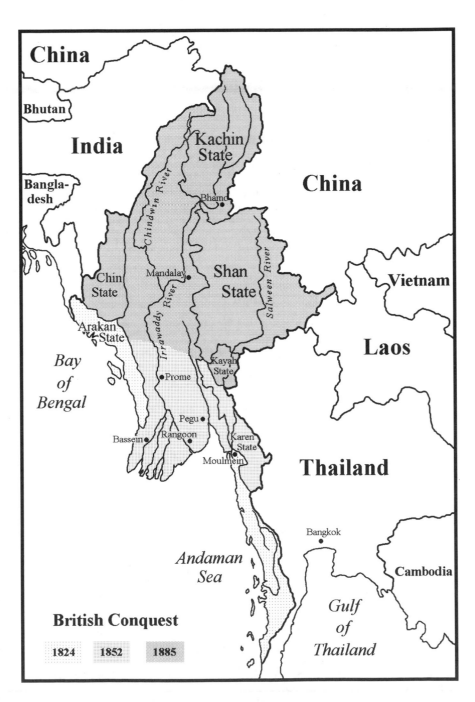

Burma Under British Control

to every good quality in the Burmese and looking through a magnifying glass at every bad characteristic."[10]

Except for missionaries, westerners went to Burma for only one reason: to make money. The social and political systems they built supported that colonial goal. They taught the Burmese to see their new rulers as superior. A British man was not addressed as an equal, using the titles *U* (literally "Uncle") or *Maung* ("Brother"). He insisted on being addressed as *Thakin*, which means "Master." The Burmese were taught that their British masters' culture was superior to their own. Interest in Burmese literature faded, and the traditional Buddhist monastic education was re-placed by missionary and government-run schools. Htin Aung stated, "Burmese boys and girls who went to the Christian schools knew more about the Ten Command-ments than the Five Precepts [of Buddhism]."[11] The new schools, however, did not prepare their students to be good citizens. The children "had not become Christians, but merely misfits in Burmese society."[12]

The British failed to recognize that their culture could not be grafted onto existing Burmese culture. In some cases, the new rulers went out of their way to tread on Burmese social customs. In little ways, the Burmese fought back with quiet defiance, trying to hold on to some of their self-respect. Though these methods may seem trivial, to a nation losing its age-old traditions they were symbolic of bigger grievances. A small but successful defiance concerned shoes. It is the height of disrespect to wear shoes in pagodas. For many years, Buddhist monks had generously over-looked the affront of western tourists wearing their shoes while sightseeing in the pagodas. As their rulers' snobbery increased, the monks fought back by strictly enforcing the no-shoes rule. Naked feet became an anti-British symbol. The British resented this, but complied.

A New Nationalism

By 1900, European colonialism in Asia was over 300 years old. Many colonies were getting restless. East of Burma, the Philippines had invited Americans to help wage war against their Spanish rulers, only to find themselves fighting a new war to avoid becoming colonial subjects of the newly arrived Americans. West as far as Africa, the Boers (themselves descended from Dutch colonists) were fighting the British. In 1905, many young Asian nationalists celebrated Japan's victory in the Russo-Japanese war. It was the first instance of an Asian people defeating a European power without outside help.

For decades, the height of ambition among many Asians under British rule had been an education in England. Many of the most successful Indian politicians and businessmen had trained in England. Motilal Nehru, a successful lawyer, sent his son Jawaharlal to study in London. Mohandas Gandhi, the son of an advisor to one of India's many local princes, went there also. When men like these returned home to apply what they had learned to their own countries, an obvious question came to mind: What gave the British, who believed in the right of each man to be his own ruler, the right to rule Indians? Unable to answer that question, the Indians concluded that the right did not exist. Nehru and Gandhi went on to lead India to independence in 1947.

World War I gave unintended aid to Asian nationalists. From the start of the war, Britain urged its colonies to join in the fight. India and even Burma raised troops to fight by England's side. In encouraging their subjects to fight, the British argued that war with the Germans was a war against oppression and for self-determination. Shrewd colonial supporters of the war accepted the British justification, for it backed the British into a corner. Come war's end, there would be some serious explaining to do. Why was German oppression bad but British "colonialism" good? In 1916, the British tried to explain. Colonial rule, Lionel Curtis said in his book *The Commonwealth of Nations*, was not forever. It was meant to guide developing nations along a steady path to political responsibility and independence. In 1917 the British Secretary of State for India announced that India (including Burma, which was officially a province of India) was heading down a one-way road to independence. The only question was, when would Burma be ready?

Burmese nationalism emerged a generation after India's, mainly because the British came later to Burma than to India. In 1886, when the Indian National Congress was formed to demand Indian rule for India, the British were only just arriving in upper Burma. It was not until 1906, when a group of western-educated Burmese formed the Young Men's Buddhist Association (YMBA), that Burmese nationalism took off. The YMBA, obviously modelled on the Young Men's Christian Association (YMCA), served as a club where politics could be learned and argued. After this, Burmese social groups sprang up everywhere. In 1920 they were united in the General Council of Burmese Associations (GCBA). With the YMBA and GCBA, as well as the Buddhist *sangha*, to lead the debate, Burmese politics matured quickly. By 1920, the Burmese were ready to follow the Indian lead of the previous generation.

The first serious clash with British rulers came in 1920, when Rangoon University students went on strike to protest entrance requirements, which they saw as an attempt to limit education to the British and the well-to-do. As the protest spread, Burmese nationalists called for a system of National Schools independent from the British-run schools. Though the National Schools failed, the students got much of what they struck for. More importantly, they set the tone for student protests that would, through the years, become the main expression of anti-government sentiment. For instance, it was Rangoon students who led the 1988 protests which resulted in mass killings by the military and Aung San Suu Kyi's arrest.

The first step toward fulfilling Britain's promise of independence came in 1923, when a new constitution took effect in India and Burma. This "Dyarchy" (literally "two governments") constitution was a new experiment. A legislature was created with some members appointed by the British Governor and some elected by the Burmese people. Some government duties, such as road maintenance and the school system, were "transferred" to a Cabinet which answered to the legislature. Other functions, such as defense and the coinage of money, were "reserved" by the British-appointed Governor. There were two governments. One elected by Burmese to handle local matters; one appointed by the British to handle national and international affairs.

Dyarchy did not work, mainly because financial matters were "reserved" for the Governor, who usually refused to provide enough money for the Cabinet to do a good job on their "transferred" duties. In 1931, London convened a Burma Round Table conference to solve the Dyarchy's problems. By the end of 1935, the British had agreed to give the people of both India and Burma more say in their governments. In 1937, a new constitution gave the Cabinet control over many matters. The Governor now directly controlled only matters which directly related to the British Empire.

The YMBA and GCBA organizations appealed mainly to Burmese familiar with the West. They had grown up speaking English, and often had been educated at Western universities. In the 1930's, organizations aimed at rural Burmese began to arise. In 1930, a former Buddhist monk named Saya San led a rebellion against the British. The uprising was easily put down, but left lingering animosities which later nationalist groups would take advantage of.

The organization which would eventually lead Burma to independence was the *Dobama Asiayone*, the "We Burmese Society." It was formed in 1935 when the All Burma Youth Group joined with the *Dobama* Society, a student group at Rangoon University. The *Dobama Asiayone* saw that the real importance of Saya San's rebellion was in awakening long-submerged dislike of British rule among the rural Burmese who had no experience with Western ideas. The *Dobama Asiayone* took ideas of freedom and democracy to Burma's villages. Its leaders would become the next generation of national leaders.

Before World War II, the *Dobama Asiayone's* actions were largely symbolic. The organization staged a strike at Rangoon University in 1936 that first brought Aung San, Suu's father, to prominence. And they stole the title *Thakin*. Members of the *Dobama Asiayone* called each other *Thakin* to protest British rule. It was their way of saying, "We are our own masters."

With the constitution of 1937, Burma was one step away from independence. No one knew how big that step was or how long the British would wait before taking it, but the Burmese were not willing to wait quietly. The YMBA, GCBA and *Dobama Asiayone* continued to demand Burma's release from British rule.

When World War II started, Britain again asked its colonies for their loyal support. This time, Burma refused, and with Burmese help, Japan invaded British Burma in late 1941, driving the British all the way to India.

World War II is a good point to leave off with Burma and take a look at Aung San Suu Kyi and her family, for it was World War II which brought *U* Aung San, and through him his daughter, to their heroic roles in Burma's history.

FOUR

AUNG SAN'S LEGACY

Aung San was born February 13, 1915, in a small village near the Irrawaddy River in central Burma. His parents were modest but well-off rural people whom he proudly called the latest in "a distinguished line of patriotic ancestors."[13] He went to the local Burmese-language high school, and then, to improve his English, to the National High School in the nearby town of Yenangyaung. After graduating high school, he attended college in Rangoon.

While at Rangoon University in the mid-1930's, Aung San was a leading instigator of the student protests there. The university expelled him in 1936 for printing an article in the student newspaper mocking one of the school's officials. Many said Aung San intentionally printed the article, titled "Hell Hound at Large," to spark trouble. If so, it worked. Aung San's expulsion launched the protests. In the end, the University backed down, and Aung San was readmitted.

After leaving Rangoon University, Aung San led the *Dobama Asiayone*, which he had joined at school. Though he helped found the Communist Party of Burma (CPB), Aung San was not a dedicated communist. Communism was defined by Karl Marx and Friedrich Engels, in their paper *The Communist Manifesto*. They argued that Capitalism, in which individual capitalists owned the means of production and reaped all the profits, was bound to give way to what they saw as a more humane system they called Communism, in which the factories and stores were owned by everyone communally and the earnings were shared by all. Many young, educated Burmese read the writings of Karl Marx with great interest. Their experiences with capitalism were limited to the extremely exploitative rule of the British, who put the profits of British capitalists first and Burmese welfare a distant second. For over one hundred years profits had flowed out of Burma into the hands of the British and the Indians. Seen in that light, Capitalism seemed extremely oppressive and Communism all the more attractive.

When conflict broke out between Great Britain and Japan in 1939, the *Thakins* of the *Dobama Asiayone* decided to take advantage of England's vulnerability. They sent Aung San to seek aid from the Chinese Communists, who were fighting the Kuomintang, or Chinese Nationalists. Though he set out seeking communist aid in China, Aung San was diverted to Japan, where he got assurances of help from the strongly anti-communist leaders there. This annoyed the devout communists in the *Dobama Asiayone*, including Aung San's future brother-in-law, *Thakin* Than Tun, and planted the seed of the communist rebellion of the late 1940's and 1950's.

After returning to Burma from Japan, Aung San assembled some of his fellow *Thakins* and returned to Japan for training in guerilla warfare. Aung San and his colleagues became the "Thirty Heros" who would lead Burma to independence. To avoid reprisals against their families, the Thirty took new names. Aung San became *Bo* Teza (Powerful General), but soon he resumed using his real name, one of the few of the Thirty who did. Another of the Thirty, an ambitious young man named *Maung* Shu Maung, took the title *Bo* Ne Win (General Sun of Glory). It seems no one at the time recognized the vanity of the young man's glorious new name. Ne Win would one day sink Burma into the depths of poverty while seeking personal glory.

While the *Thakins* trained in Japan, Burma's Prime Minister, *U* Saw, travelled to London seeking a promise of independence if Burma supported England in its war. Unknown to the British, the Japanese had already promised Burma immediate independence in exchange for Burmese aid in expelling the British from southeast Asia. London refused *U* Saw's request, thus guaranteeing that Burma would side with Japan in the war.

At the end of 1941, the Thirty Heroes returned to Burma beside the invading Japanese. Within months the Japanese drove the British out of Burma.

But the *Thakins* soon grew disillusioned with their Japanese allies, for their promise of independence was quickly broken. A Japanese occupational government ruled throughout 1942. The next year Burma was granted a limited independence under a pro-Japanese fascist government which was little more than a puppet government for the Japanese army, which stayed in Burma. In 1944, in response to Japan's broken promise, the *Thakins* formed an anti-Japanese organization, the Anti-Fascist People's Freedom League (AFPFL), with Aung San at its head. The AFPFL spent the next three years planning and waiting.

It was during those years, when he was hospitalized with malaria, that Aung San met *Ma* (Miss) Khin Kyi. The daughter of a Christian father and Buddhist mother, Khin Kyi was a trained nurse. She nursed the handsome young general back to health. Within months they were married, and began a family.

Aung San of Burma, circa 1945

March 1945 was a tumultuous time in Rangoon, the capital of Japanese-occupied Burma. Rumors floated throughout the city that the Burmese army was up to mischief. North of the city along the road from Mandalay, British and Japanese armies fought fiercely. If Japanese defenses could hold out until May, the monsoons would start, stalling British supply lines under unending rain and mud that forced the British to retreat all the way back into India.

On March 26, *Daw* Khin Kyi, now the wife of General Aung San and the mother of two young sons, left her home and disappeared into hiding. At the time she was six months pregnant with her third child. The next day, the Burmese army, led by *Bo* (General) Aung San, attacked the Japanese from the rear, a move that stunned the occupiers. The strong Japanese defenses collapsed, and the battle became a rout. The road to Rangoon was open. The day Aung San struck, March 27, has been celebrated in Burma as Armed Forces Day ever since.

By May, when the rains started, Rangoon was free and Aung San's family could emerge from hiding. Aung San entered the city a national hero for leading the crushing defeat of the Japanese. He was christened *Bogyoke*, or Great General. Burma was again a British colony.

FIVE

A QUIET YOUNG WOMAN

Just one month after the British reentered Rangoon, on Tuesday, June 19, 1945, *Daw* Khin Kyi gave birth to her third child and first daughter. Aung San named his daughter Aung San Suu Kyi (pronounced Aung Sahn Sue Chee). Aung San for her father. Suu for her paternal grandmother. Kyi for her mother. Burmese astrology would predict that, being Tuesday-born, the child would have an honest character. Mya Maung, a Burmese writer, says the name means a "successful, extraordinary, pure and clear" person.[14] Suu herself says it means "a bright collection of strange victories."[15]

With the war winding down, Aung San would have liked to settle in with his young family. Three years earlier, when he had married *Ma* Khin Kyi, his colleagues had worried he would retire from the political turmoil Burma faced. But Aung San was too deeply involved to let events pass him by.

Returning from India after British troops retook Burma in 1945, Governor-General Dorman-Smith declared Aung San a traitor to the British Empire. Dorman-Smith placed the young hero at the top of a list of people to be arrested "On sight." For a while Aung San went into hiding. But Lord Louis Mountbatten, commander of the British army in Burma, intervened. Mountbatten recognized Aung San's role in beating the Japanese. What's more, he saw how the people revered their *Bogyoke* (Great General), and knew his arrest might cause the Burmese to revolt. Mountbatten refused to allow Aung San's arrest, and London backed his decision.

Aung San was not free from arrest for long, however. In March 1946 Dorman-Smith again tried to have him arrested, this time charging him with the murder of a village headman in 1942. Again the government in London stopped the arrest before it happened. The charge was never tried.

After his legal troubles subsided, Aung San still could not live a quiet life with his family. At the end of the war, Aung San built a military wing for the AFPFL, the People's Volunteer Organization (PVO). The threat was clear: if England won't negotiate, we'll fight. But England knew that colonial rule in Asia was over. In August, 1946, London sent Sir Hubert Rance to replace the intractable Dorman-Smith, who refused to negotiate with Aung San, by then the clear leader of the Burmese. Within a few months an agreement was signed, and Aung San boarded a ship to London to negotiate the formal treaty of independence with Prime Minister Clement Attlee.

During quiet times in London, Aung San would softly sing songs with his friends and tell stories about his family in Rangoon. His friends gave him presents to take home, books for the older children or dolls for the one-year-old Suu.

On January 27, 1947, Attlee and Aung San signed an agreement that would grant Burma independence within a year. This promise would be kept. Burma would become independent at 4:20 a.m. on January 4, 1948, a time and date the stars favored.

Aung San, now head of the transition government, returned to Burma triumphant. The end of his troubles—Burma's troubles—was near. Finally he could spend some time with his family. *Daw* Khin Kyi had given birth to a second daughter the autumn before, a few months before Aung San left for England, but the child had died. The infant's death seems to have affected Aung San strongly. He recognized that he could lose all his children, perhaps to death but certainly to the passage of time. He did not want to be an absentee father, always away from home. As soon as independence was complete, Aung San wanted to retire from politics, write books, and help raise his family. Though he had fought against British rule in Burma, he was not anti-British. He wanted Burma, like the United States and many former British colonies, to build strong ties of friendship to its former rulers. His arts degree from Rangoon University had concentrated on English literature and modern history, and he had developed a strong love of English literature and an admiration for the British way of government. This was part of the heritage he wanted to pass on to his children.

He settled into a regular routine, travelling the country-side giving speeches and working out the details of the new Burmese government, which everyone assumed he would lead. The family lived in a turreted colonial house on Tower Lane, a quiet, tree-lined road near the center of Rangoon. As often as possible, Khin Kyi and the children joined him on his trips, bringing a semblance of home life to this man who had been a wanderer for almost ten years. When their parents were working, the children would often be put in the care of Aung San's military aides.

But Aung San was not destined to see Burma become free. Nor would the wandering father see his two-year-old daughter grow up. A few months before Burma was to become independent, *U* Saw, Burma's Prime Minister before the war and an old political rival of Aung San, caught up with him. As Aung San held a Cabinet meeting in

Rangoon, his rival's gunmen stormed into the room. The meeting erupted in chaos. Aung San and his associates scrambled for cover as the gunmen sprayed shots through the room. When the shooting stopped, Burma's future had changed forever. Aung San, the one man who people believed could unite the country, and most of his Cabinet, were dead. *U* Nu, who survived the assassination, became Burma's Prime Minister; he would be the only democratically-elected Prime Minister the country would have. Some people viewed *U* Saw's attack as a throwback to the days of the Burmese Kingdom, when all a *minlawn*, or pretender to the throne, had to do was assassinate the king and claim the throne. Perhaps *U* Saw thought he could become Prime Minister by assassinating Aung San, though more likely he was simply getting even for a grudge he held. Whatever his motives, *U* Saw, the man who ordered Aung San's killing, was arrested, tried, and executed.

Khin Kyi was a strong woman, not one to be easily discouraged. A soldier's wife must always be prepared for her husband's sudden death. She immediately started rebuilding her life.

Now that Aung San was dead, his widow assumed his seat in parliament. Khin Kyi was not the first woman to be active in Burmese politics. Many of the kings were closely advised by their queens. In some cases, it is not unreasonable to say the queen had held the real power. Before King Minkyinyo reunited Burma for the Second Unification, the independent Mon Kingdom at Pegu had a female "King," Shin Saw Bu. More recently, *Daw* Mya Sein had participated in the 1932 Burma Round Table conference in London and had been an emissary to China in 1939-40. *Ma* Than E, a family friend, was a student in London when Aung San negotiated independence. She went on to a distinguished career at the United Nations.

Daw Khin Kyi, however, did not stay in parliament long. Nursing, not politics, was her real interest. She soon resigned to become chairman of the Council of Social Services, a post she held many years. Khin Kyi was dedicated to her work.

But tragedy continued to dog *Daw* Khin Kyi. Years later Suu told the story of her brother's death. Suu was very close to Aung San Lin, the brother nearest to her own age. A bright boy who absorbed his lessons on first reading, he was also a daring and mischievous youngster who played pranks and got himself into innocuous trouble—sometimes with his little sister Suu, who adored him. Perhaps it was this daring nature that cost him his life. Khin Kyi was in a conference at work when the news reached her that Aung San Lin had drowned in a pond near the house. Though she loved her family dearly, Khin Kyi never let her personal tragedies interrupt the duty she felt she owed Burma. She took the tragic news stoically, insisting on finishing her day's work before going to see her son's body.

After Aung San Lin's drowning, the old colonial house on Tower Lane held too many tragic memories for *Daw* Khin Kyi and her family. They moved to a large, newly-built house on the shore of Inya Lake in the north of Rangoon.

Suu's mother provided a strong, stable home for the children to grow up in. But, with their father dead and their mother working full time, Suu and her brother fell under the care of the bevy of aunts and uncles who actually ran the household.

Khin Kyi insisted that the children grow up knowing the life of their late father. Though Aung San was killed at a mere 32 years of age, he had achieved amazing feats. Few who knew him failed to admire and respect the man. Many said he had a knack for turning bitter enemies into fast friends. Chin and Karen leaders in parliament said Aung San was the one Burman whom they could trust absolutely. This was the father Aung San's widow wanted her children to know: a man of absolute devotion to a united Burma. Each month as Suu was growing up, their mother held a memorial for their father in the house, led by Buddhist monks from the monastery near the old house on Tower Lane.

Suu Kyi at six years of age.

Aung San and *Daw* Khin Kyi had always taught their children that Burma's ethnic groups could live peaceably together. To Suu's parents, it was certain that Burman, Chin, Karen, Shan, Mon, and all the rest could build a strong country together. Khin Kyi practiced the same democracy in her own home. The house was constantly filled with visitors. "From my earliest childhood," Suu said, "my mother taught me this idea of national unity. [We] always had people from various ethnic groups living with us."[16] Nursing students from all parts of the country were welcomed into Khin Kyi's home, often staying with the family for long periods. Suu absorbed stories and customs from many different Burmese people. Though Suu and her brother were raised as devout Buddhists, their Christian grandfather taught them to respect different religions. When her grandfather grew old, Suu would sit in the evening and read the Bible to him in Burmese.

Politics, of course, permeated the house. Though Aung San and *U* Ba Win, one of his brothers, had been killed, many of the family friends were old comrades from the war years. Another brother of Aung San, *U* Aung Than, led a political party. *Daw* Khin Kyi's brother-in-law, *Thakin* Than Tun, led a communist group which had been expelled from the AFPFL for being too revolutionary. With her father, mother, and uncles for examples, there was much to impress a feeling of civic obligation to Burma on the young Suu. She was always aware that, as Aung San's daughter, she had a special obligation to her country, though no one ever said exactly what that obligation was.

Even if Khin Kyi had not taught her children of their father's life, they could hardly have forgotten him. When she grew older, Suu could stroll down *Bogyoke* Aung San Street, right up from Anawrahta Street. She could shop at the enormous *Bogyoke* Aung San Market, or visit the Aung San museum on Tower Lane across from the house she lived in when she was young. She could cool her feet in the pond at *Bogyoke* Aung San Park on the way home.

Suu was sent to the best private school in Rangoon, the English Methodist High School. Formed during colonial days as a missionary school, the school educated all the children of Rangoon's elite. Though a Christian missionary school, the curriculum tried to teach Christianity without interfering with the students' Buddhist beliefs. Burmese culture was no longer considered inherently inferior. In fact, despite the school's name, the language used for everyday instruction was Burmese.

Suu was already a dedicated reader. *U* Ohn, a former journalist who had worked with her father in London, put together Burmese and English reading lists for the young woman, and kept her supplied with piles of books.

In 1960, while Suu was still in high school, her mother was appointed Burmese Ambassador to India, the first Burmese woman to hold such a high post in the fourteen years of independence. That year Aung San U, Suu's older brother, left to study in England, and Suu went with her mother to New Delhi. Mother and daughter lived in a magnificent colonial home which had been built for high Indian officials.

In New Delhi, Suu finished high school at the Convent of Jesus and Mary, a private school run by Irish Catholic nuns. She was a quiet girl, who had close friends but did not join many school clubs, though she once wrote a parody of Shakespeare's *Anthony and Cleopatra*, which the drama club put on one semester. While finishing high school, she took horse riding lessons from members of the Indian Presidential bodyguard, and learned to play the piano. Her home life, which had brought her in contact with the most prominent figures of Burmese politics, now expanded even more. She met many prominent Indians such as Rajiv Gandhi, Indira Gandhi's son and Jawaharlal Nehru's grandson. Both Indira and Rajiv went on to be Prime Ministers of India.

Although she met many high government officials through her mother's post as Ambassador, Suu felt closer to more ordinary people. She made her longest lasting friendships among her Indian classmates. She never grew very close to Rajiv Gandhi or his brother, and drifted away from them after leaving New Delhi, but she has kept in lifelong touch with several of her less prominent classmates.

Suu continued to read voraciously. She went through everything from Greek mythology to English literature, and avidly devoured long-neglected Burmese poetry and novels from the days of the Kingdom.

The move to India helped to focus Suu's political awareness. India's Prime Minister Nehru had been a friend of her father during India's and Burma's fights for independence in the 1930's and 1940's. In New Delhi the family friendship was renewed. Suu looked up to Nehru as an example of a practical idealist, someone who could blend the idealism of a Gandhi with the shrewdness necessary for politics.

Already Suu was writing school papers with titles such as "What is Democracy?" Perhaps the reading most influential to Suu's growing political awareness was the life and works of Mohandas K. Gandhi. Gandhi had been the most influential activist for Indian independence. For his lifelong dedication to improving the conditions of Indians, Gandhi came to be called "Mahatma," which means "Great Soul". From the start, Gandhi had practiced only non-violent means to achieve his political goals. Suu, already prejudiced against violence by her father's murder, was permanently won over to Gandhi's non-violent approach to politics. "My father died because there were people who preferred guns to solve political problems," she later said.[17]

SIX

SCHOLAR, WIFE, AND MOTHER

After high school Suu for a time attended Lady Sri Ram College. But her ambition was to study at Oxford, a university she saw as offering the best education available. She began studying the "advanced" level General Certificate of Education courses required to meet the strict entrance requirements for Oxford University. She quickly absorbed the material in the courses, finishing, for example, a two-year mathematics course in just a few months. In 1964, Suu left for Oxford, one of the first Burmese to be accepted for an undergraduate degree there. Sir (later Lord) Paul Gore-Booth, who became a close family friend when he served as British Ambassador to Burma, and his wife Patricia took the quiet young Burmese woman under their wing, introducing her to their wide circle of friends in public life. While at Oxford she spent many evenings at the Gore-Booth home, listening and learning. With her Burmese, Indian, and now British experiences, she was becoming quite a woman of the world.

Ann Pasternak Slater, niece of the Russian author Boris Pasternak, was one of Suu's close friends at Oxford.[18] In 1964, the university was at the beginning of the sexual revolution that would transform many college campuses in both England and the United States. "By the popular morality of the time," Ann Slater recalled, "Suu was a pure oriental traditionalist. Even the way she held herself was instinctively straight-laced." In part, Suu cultivated this image. She was proud of her Burmese heritage and wanted people to know so. In the days of mini-skirts, Suu insisted on wearing traditional Burmese *lungyis*, close-fitting wrap-around skirts which hang to the wearer's ankles. She could be seen wearing her *lungyi* out on the pond learning to row a punt, a canoe-like boat. Suu finally bought a pair of jeans to wear when she learned to ride a bicycle.

"At the same time," Ann Slater remembers, "she was curious to experience the European and the alien." Finally, in her senior year, Suu decided to "experience" alcohol. "In great secrecy, she bought a miniature bottle—of what? sherry? wine?—and, with two rather more worldly Indians, retired to the ladies' lavatory in the Bodleian Library. There, among the sinks and the cubicles, in a setting deliberately chosen to mirror the distastefulness of the experience, she tried and rejected alcohol forever."

Suu's "rebellions" may seem tame and timid compared to the wild happenings on college campuses in later years, but for her they were a real change from the rigid life she had lived in the public eye in Rangoon and as an ambassador's daughter in New Delhi.

But Suu was not at Oxford to hobnob with British gentry or to experiment with the petty vices of a different culture. She was a serious student, studying Politics, Philosophy, and Economics (known as PPE), a degree course designed for students preparing themselves for leadership roles. She delved into her studies, absorbing the philosophy behind liberal western democracy.

Though she would have preferred to take her degree in English Literature or Forestry, Suu's feeling of obligation to Burma overruled her own preference. While she was in India, Burma's democracy had collapsed. The constitution of 1948 allowed the minorities along Burma's borders to secede after a ten year period. When 1958 arrived, the Shans in eastern Burma began rallying for their own independent state. Prime Minister U Nu negotiated with the Shans as well as the Kachins in northern Burma, trying to keep them in the union. By 1962 it was clear the Shans were serious about leaving Burma. *Bo* Ne Win, the "Sun of Glory" General, used the possible disintegration of the Burmese union as a pretext to seize power. On March 2, 1962, Ne Win overthrew Burma's elected government.

To Suu it was obvious that after the army relinquished power, which everyone hoped would happen quickly, Burma would be in need of a new generation of young, vigorous politicians like the *Thakins* of the 1930's. To some extent, she may have seen herself filling that role, like her father before her.

In addition to political turmoil, Burma faced severe economic problems. "Economics seemed to be of most use for a developing country," Suu said, explaining her decision to major in PPE.[19] By the early 1960's, Burma had still not recovered from the heavy destruction of World War II. This was the problem that urged Suu into a PPE curriculum.

At Oxford, as in New Delhi, Suu avoided school orga- nizations. Part of the reason was that for her, as Aung San's daughter, joining organizations could easily be seen as a political statement. But also, her personality made her shy away from group activities. She preferred to build her friendships one-on-one. She did practice her speaking and debating skills at Gore-Booth's home, and joined the Oxford Union debating society, although apparently she did not participate in many of the group's activities. She paid close attention to the American civil rights movement, becoming an admirer of Dr. Martin Luther King Jr, who in many ways reinforced her belief in non-violence. She also followed the Vietnam protests. She seems to have sided with those who felt the US had no business in Vietnam in the first place, but generally she kept her opinions to herself, not participating in public protests.

Suu also avoided the activities of the Burmese community in Oxford. She did not want to give the impression that she supported Ne Win's government by joining government-sponsored groups, nor that she would oppose the government from a secure, safe stage in England. "I would never do anything from abroad," Suu said years later. "If I were to engage in any political movement I would do so from within the country."[20]

During summer break, Suu usually returned to her mother's home in New Delhi. One year, however, she rested by spending the summer in Algeria studying the civil unrest which had erupted there. She took trips throughout northern Africa and to Spain, and spent her spare time helping to build homes in Algiers for widows of the Algerian fighting.

The PPE curriculum seems to have failed to meet Suu's expectations. Both the philosophy and economics taught struck her as too theoretical and impractical to help with Burma's problems. She searched for more useful areas to study. For a time she considered agriculture and forestry, and even medicine. Twice she tried to change her major, to Forestry and then to English Literature, but both times was turned down because of Oxford's strict rules against such changes.

After graduating from Oxford with honors in 1967, Suu was at a bit of a loss about what to do. She taught at an English preparatory school for a year, teaching high school age students, and worked as a research assistant for Hugh Tinker, a Burma scholar at London University's School of Oriental and Asian Studies. Finally, in 1969, she went to New York City, hoping to launch a career at the United Nations. There she shared an apartment with *Ma* Than E, an old family friend she had stayed with in Algiers. For a while Suu also studied English literature at New York University. *Ma* Than E was then an employee of the United Nations in New York. After trying several jobs, Suu settled into a job with the UN Advisory Committee on Administrative and Budgetary Questions, a position which made good use of her PPE background. In addition to her work and continuing studies, Suu found time to volunteer at New York's Bellevue Hospital. Compared to Oxford, New York can seem a cruel and harsh place. Bellevue, a city-run hospital, takes many of the city's most impoverished, desperate people in need of medical help. Suu—along with

*U Thant, in a 1965 photo. As Secretary-General
of the United Nations, he was one of
the first Burmese to achieve international
prominence.* (United Nations)

other generous New Yorkers—provided desperately needed companionship to that institution's poor and hopeless patients who literally had no one to listen to them.

While in New York, Suu found time between work, school, and volunteerism to take in concerts at Lincoln Center and other cultural attractions. At that time, the Burmese community at the UN was especially strong. *U* Thant, a genial former official in *U* Nu's government, was then UN Secretary-General. Many Burmese spent long hours socializing in the Secretary-General's home. Suu also travelled up the East coast to see Boston, and down to Washington D.C. Once, her desire to see different people and places led her to board a Greyhound bus to "see America." She rode cross-country all the way to California.

Suu stayed at the UN for three years. In 1971, she seemed dedicated to a career in the United Nations. But then she abruptly changed course. Almost ten years earlier Christopher Gore-Booth, the son of Paul and Patricia Gore-Booth, had introduced Michael Aris, a friend at Durham University in London, to Suu. Aris had an avid interest in Asia. Alongside his formal degree in history, he studied Tibetan culture, and after graduation, went to the small, landlocked country of Bhutan, located northwest of Burma, where he took the job of tutor to the Bhutanese royal family. In the years after college, Michael and Suu had kept in touch by letter. Gradually, their love grew. In 1970, Suu took a trip to visit Michael. They travelled through Bhutan together. When Suu returned to the United States, she and Michael Aris were engaged. Throughout 1971 they wrote almost daily letters to each other from halfway across the world. On New Year's Day, 1972, they were married.

After marriage, Suu left her job at the UN to be with Michael in Bhutan. Though she left her budding career in the United Nations behind for marriage, Suu could not leave behind her obligation to Burma. She knew Ne Win's vice-like grip on the country could not last forever. "When I married Michael," Suu said in an interview in 1988, "I made him promise that if there was ever a time I had to go back to my country, he would not stand in my way. And he promised."[21]

The newlyweds settled in Bhutan for almost two years, Suu taking a job with the Bhutanese Foreign Ministry. In 1973 they returned to England for the birth of their first son, and set up house in a small apartment in London, where Michael began work on his doctorate. They named the boy Alexander. Four years later, in 1977, Michael and Suu had another son, Kim.

In 1976 the family moved to Oxford, and the next half-dozen years passed swiftly in that quiet college town. Much

Suu Kyi with husband Michael Aris in 1973.
(Sygma/Ira Wyman)

as had her own mother, Suu entertained a constant stream of household visitors. Though all she and Michael could afford was a small apartment, in Ann Slater's eyes they "welcomed and uncomplainingly entertained for punishing periods," Burmese and Bhutanese friends, and Suu's visiting relatives. Finally, though the extra cost was a burden, the couple moved into a larger house in a "shabby-genteel" neighborhood in Oxford, as much to accommodate their friends as themselves.[22]

Suu remained fascinated by reading and by learning. Even the rearing of two young children, and entertaining hordes of friends and guests could not fill the days of this energetic young woman. She reapplied to Oxford to work on a degree in English, but was not admitted. Undaunted, she started on another project: a biography of Aung San. *Daw* Khin Kyi had left Suu with an enduring desire to know her father. Suu had gathered material about him for years, and now she organized her collection and finished the project. Her first book, titled simply *Aung San*, was published in 1984. Still, she did not stop studying her father's life. She applied for and won a scholarship to the University of Kyoto, in Japan. In 1985, after teaching herself to speak Japanese, Suu and Kim left Oxford for Japan, to gather papers on Aung San's trips there in 1941-2 and to interview those who had known her father. When she finished there, she rejoined Michael and Alexander in Simla, India, where Michael was a visiting Fellow at the Indian Institute for Advanced Studies.

In September 1987, the entire family returned to Oxford, where Michael continued his writings on Tibet and the Himalayas. After returning to England, Suu wrote a short history of her homeland titled *Let's Visit Burma*, two more books on Nepal and Bhutan, and scholarly papers about Burmese and Indian literature during colonial times. Then, in 1988, Suu applied and was accepted to the graduate school at London University's School of Oriental and Asian Studies. She planned to write her doctoral dissertation on Burmese literature.

Suu might have remained a quiet, scholarly woman, mother of two growing boys and wife of an Oxford scholar, but for the conjunction of two unrelated events. On March 31, 1988, Suu received a phone call from Rangoon. Her mother, *Daw* Khin Kyi, had suffered a severe stroke. Suu immediately packed and flew to her mother's side at Rangoon General Hospital. The other event was a petty brawl in a teahouse just off the campus of the Rangoon Institute of Technology.

SEVEN

UNREST IN BURMA BEGINS

The brawl that was to change Suu's future occurred on March 12, 1988, more than two weeks before she arrived in Burma. No one knows for sure what started it. One version says it began as an argument over what music to play on the radio. Some people think it began over a political argument. A third, equally likely theory, is that the fight started over a gambling debt.

Everyone agrees on the events of the fight, if not its cause. It happened in a teahouse near the Rangoon Institute of Technology (RIT). Several RIT students argued with the son of the teahouse owner. He pulled out a knife and one of the students, Win Myint, was stabbed. The RIT students reported the assault to the police and retreated to campus to tend their comrade's wound. Back on campus, Win Myint's friends gathered around him to hear his story.

The next day Win Myint's assailant was released from jail. Many students feared the incident would be whitewashed and Win Myint's assailant would go unpunished, for his father was a member of the *Myanma Sosialit Lanzin Pati* (the "Burma Socialist Program Party"), which dictator Ne Win formed when he took control, and also a member of the local governing "People's Council". Known as the *Lanzins* by its members and called *Ma Sa La* (for its initials M-S-L) by almost everyone else, the Burma Socialist Program Party was Burma's only legal political party.

A small but angry crowd gathered in front of the People's Council, demanding apologies and compensation from the teashop's owner and his son. It became obvious trouble was brewing when *Lon Htein*, Burma's riot police, showed up.

The appearance of the riot police was not the best way to defuse the confrontation. Students saw the *Lon Htein* as stooges of the ruling party, and expected no justice from them. The students suddenly redirected their anger toward the police. After the *Lon Htein* arrived, the crowd quickly degenerated into an angry mob, throwing rocks and bottles. The police responded with clubs and, when the angry crowd did not break up, with gunshots. One student, *Maung* Phone Maw, was killed.

The student's death touched off the unrest that had been

threatening Rangoon. By 1988, many of Burma's people, especially the young students, were opponents of the military. *Ma Sa La's* "Burmese Way to Socialism," a self-contradictory combination of Buddhism and Marxism (which denies religion), had been the guiding principle for the Burmese economy for a quarter century. There was little or no future for a college graduate in Burma, in large part because of *Ma Sa La's* mismanagement of the economy. The final, most disheartening blow to Burma's economic future had come in late 1987, when the government devalued much of Burma's currency, making it worthless, and making the lives of Burma's struggling poor even more wretched. The UN had placed Burma, once southeast Asia's richest nation, on its "Least Developed Nations" list. All these events had created a deep despair among Burma's youth, especially those who had attended college and now discovered there were no jobs waiting for them after years of work. The streets of Rangoon were a tinderbox. These conditions were what turned a petty fight in a teashop into a public protest against the government.

That evening, using *Maung* Phone Maw's bloody shirt as a banner, angry students held a rally, demanding compensation for the dead boy's family, and a State funeral— a hero's funeral. The students also demanded economic reform to create opportunities for university graduates.

Tacked onto the end of their list of demands, like an afterthought, was one last demand: Democracy. Clearly, the death of *Maung* Phone Maw had become a symbol for the years of pent-up frustration among Burma's youth.

The *Lon Htein* responded forcefully to the student's challenge. On March 15, the police stormed the campus of the Rangoon Institute of Technology to break up the demonstrations, beating and arresting large numbers of students.

The students should have expected the severe crackdown. The government had shown how brutally it would respond to protests many times before. Earlier, when the students at Rangoon University had met to protest Ne Win's seizure of power, the government had broken the demonstrations and demolished the Student Union building as punishment. Another time, when UN Secretary-General *U* Thant's body was returned to Burma, students demanding a proper funeral had been attacked. Estimates of the dead in that incident went as high as 1000.

The day after the attack at the Rangoon Institute of Technology, students from Rangoon University joined the protests to support their comrades at the Institute. The university students assembled and started walking up Prome Road from the Rangoon campus toward the Institute.

They never made it. The road between the two campuses

follows long, winding Inya Lake. The marching students were met by government forces on a small peninsula jutting into the lake. Frightened students began singing to bolster their courage. When it became clear they could not go forward, the students tried to retreat—only to find armed troops behind them also. They were trapped.

According to the government, no violence occurred that day. But eyewitnesses tell a different story. The police and army troops charged, firing into the crowd and swinging clubs at stragglers. Aung Gyi, who would soon become a leader of the opposition, claimed the *Lon Htein* concentrated their blows on the girls in the crowd, and beat people kneeling to pray or begging for mercy. The students panicked. The riot police drove fleeing students toward a white bridge at the end of the peninsula. The bridge was closed off, trapping the young people, who were driven to the shore of Inya Lake. But, according to eyewitnesses, the army did not stop there. Students, some of whom could not swim, were driven into the lake to drown. Some eyewitnesses claimed to have seen police holding students' heads under water until they were dead.

No accurate count of the dead was ever made. The students, dubbing the incident the White Bridge Massacre, claimed over a hundred were slaughtered on land, with perhaps two dozen more drowned and disappeared in the waters of Inya Lake. The next day female students, beaten and bleeding, showed up at Rangoon General Hospital and said they had been raped by the police. The students rechristened the white bridge red, for the innocent blood spilled there. But the government continued to deny that violence had taken place.

Protests continued to grow. On March 17, thousands of people gathered for *Maung* Phone Maw's funeral, only to learn that the government had earlier secretly cremated the body. The crowd then reassembled at Rangoon University, where the *Lon Htein* arrested about one thousand of them, and sent them to Rangoon's Insein Prison, notorious for its brutal conditions.

On March 18, the unrest overflowed the college campuses. Students marching through downtown Rangoon to a rally at Sule Pagoda were joined by Rangoon residents. The government, fearful of a general uprising, declared the universities closed and called in the *Lon Htein*, and three army Divisions, to crush the protests. In a battle that lasted all day, hundreds of protesters were wounded. Many of the wounded later died, and again large numbers of protesters were taken to prison.

The March 18 fighting had the effect the government sought. The violence was so great that, faced with massive killings, the protests subsided. With the schools closed, students had to take refuge elsewhere. Many returned to their home towns. Some sought refuge on the grounds of Rangoon's Shwedagon Pagoda, Burma's most revered Buddhist shrine. The students dubbed the fight "Bloody Friday," and tagged Sein Lwin, the head of the *Lon Htein*, with a nickname: The Butcher of Burma.

The unrest had subsided completely by early April, when Suu arrived at Rangoon General Hospital to tend her mother. Although the government thought it had the situation well under control, it was merely the lull before the coming storm.

Inside the hospital room, *Daw* Khin Kyi's health steadily deteriorated. Her stroke had left her partially paralyzed, and she required constant nursing care. For the next three months Suu lived and slept by her mother's side, tending the dying woman and watching the unrest grow. As protesters were attacked and evicted from their meeting places, they sought new, safer places to meet. One popular site was the grounds in front of the U.S. Embassy. They thought, correctly, that the riot police would be less brutal in full view of the Americans, who were providing money and arms for Burma's war on the opium trade. Rangoon General Hospital (Main), a place of healing, was another preferred site for protests. However, Suu and her mother stayed in a branch of Rangoon General Hospital some distance away from most of the riots.

Early in June, the government issued its official report on the March violence. According to the report, six hundred had been arrested and three rioters had died.

Others who were present told a different story. All eyewitnesses agreed that more than three protesters had died at the white bridge. Arrested students fared little better than those who were shot or drowned. In one single incident, 42 arrested students suffocated in an overcrowded police van. Those released from Insein Prison reported that prisoners were being mutilated, raped, and tortured with electric cattle prods.

The week before the March violence began, an ex-general named Aung Gyi, whom Ne Win had thrown out of the army and imprisoned for several years, had written and published a long letter to Ne Win, warning that economic problems would soon lead to civil unrest. Ne Win had ignored the letter.

On May 30, believing the situation was well under control, the government reopened Burma's universities. Student leaders immediately began publicizing their experiences in Insein Prison. Now, in early June, Aung Gyi wrote again warning that Burma faced mass unrest, perhaps civil war, if *Ma Sa La* did nothing to correct the failures of "the Burmese Way to Socialism." This time Aung Gyi warned that the situation had gone beyond economics. The nation demanded—and deserved—a complete account of the March unrest, especially *Lon Htein's* role in human rights abuses.

Ne Win continued to ignore Aung Gyi's advice, steadily maintaining that the March protests were isolated incidents brought on by hoodlums. The next week, Rangoon University students went further, issuing an ultimatum: If a full account was not published by June 17, there would be "trouble."

On June 17, the universities were again closed. But the students did not disperse. Three days later, they kept their word and held a rally on the Rangoon University campus. Thousands of students gathered. But more importantly, they were joined by thousands of other citizens, including high-schoolers and factory workers. The Institute of Medicine in downtown Rangoon joined in the protests. Significantly, for the first time Buddhist monks joined in the rallies, violating a ban on political involvement of the *sangha* dating from before Anawrahta's time.

It is unclear if the protesters discussed their plans with

Suu at this time, but it is unlikely. From her room in Rangoon General Hospital she surely knew what was happening—she may have seen much of it first hand. The protesters had no real plan, other than to fight the government, and they had no real leader. Certainly, Suu did not actively direct them, for she strongly opposed the violent path some of the students were about to take. In cities, from Moulmein in the south, to Pegu and Prome north of Rangoon, demonstrations erupted spontaneously. Textile factory workers, on hearing of the protests, walked off their jobs in support of the students. But no one leader was coordinating the events, and no single figure expressed the protesters' demands.

On the evening of June 20, the *Lon Htein* sealed off the university. The next day, protesters took to the streets. This time they were armed. When *Lon Htein* attacked, the protesters fought back with *jinglees*, homemade slingshots which fired sharpened bicycle spokes. All the remaining schools in Rangoon and Mandalay were closed that day. All public gatherings were banned. Instead of dispersing, as they had in March, the students fled to the Shwedagon Pagoda.

Over the next month, battles were fought between the government troops and protesters armed with *jinglees*. On July 23, Ne Win attempted to quell the trouble by announcing his resignation, and calling for a referendum on democratic reform. There was dancing in the streets of Rangoon. To all appearances, the protesters had won. But over the next few days the joy evaporated. The proposed referendum was soundly defeated by *Ma Sa La's* special congress, and, after fierce debate, Ne Win was "allowed" to resign. The party chose Sein Lwin, the infamous "Butcher of Burma," as its new chairman.

The euphoria of July 23 immediately dissipated. With Ne Win's close friend at the helm, there had been no real change. The "Sun of Glory" dictator, even stripped of office, would still wield great influence, if not outright power. And even if Ne Win truly retired, Sein Lwin was perhaps the only man Burma hated more than Ne Win.

To Suu, however, Ne Win's resignation was the event she had been anticipating for years. There had been unrest in Burma before, most notably when Ne Win seized power in 1962, and when Burma's struggling economy began its final disintegration in the early 1980's. But this time Suu thought things were different. With students, workers, and the *sangha* united in their calls for reform, and with Ne Win's recognition that he must eventually pass power to others, Suu saw the opportunity she had warned her husband about nearly twenty years before. It was time for Aung San's daughter to give something back to her country.

At first, Suu's involvement in the political struggle was

limited. Her primary duty was to her mother, who, after three months in the hospital, was clearly not going to recover. Suu brought her mother home to die in the comfort of her home, surrounded by her family and friends.

Once established in the house on University Avenue, Suu transformed the home into a political center. She began meeting with the students and *sangha*, as well as emerging opposition leaders. *U* Aung Gyi and *U* Tin U, two generals whom Ne Win had fired and at various times jailed, were growing into respected leaders of the movement. *U* Nu, the Prime Minister whom Ne Win deposed, also joined the movement for democracy.

Though she discussed the direction the movement should go with her fellow leaders, Suu still did not join any of the political parties they formed. She insisted on staying aloof from partisan politics. Once someone joined a party, she argued, he or she could be reduced to a label. Opponents could attack individuals through their party. If one radical or communist joined a party, *Ma Sa La* could attack every member of that party for "associating" with radicals, communists—or anyone else they did not like. She wanted to avoid the name calling which allows each side to brand its opponents "Liberals" and "Right-wingers", "Communists" and "Fascists."

Suu discussed taking a greater public role with her

husband, who had brought their sons to Rangoon at the end of the Oxford school year. It was not an easy decision. No matter what Ne Win might say, it appeared unlikely that any true reform would take place. *Ma Sa La* had a 26-year track record of undisguised brutality, and the latest, bloodiest chapters had been written in March and June. Any political action was dangerous. It would have been very easy for Suu simply to wait out her mother's illness and return to the safety of her studies.

But returning to England while Burma burned was never a real option. Suu could not just sit by and watch what was happening. Her decision to join the movement "was prompted partly by the belief that as my father's daughter I have a responsibility towards my country."[23]

Suu's message to the students grew from her lifelong commitment to non-violence. She stressed that a new Burma could not be founded merely on opposition to Ne Win, *Ma Sa La*, *Lon Htein*, or the army. A democratic Burma could not be won with *jinglees*. Just as her father had argued that he was neither anti-British nor anti-Japanese, but rather pro-Burmese, Suu argued that a new Burma must be founded on what the protesters were *for*, not what they were against.

As her mother's health deteriorated through July and August, Suu remained a coach on the sidelines rather than a player in the political game. She encouraged the protesters to look to the future and to concentrate on creating democratic institutions rather than ousting Ne Win or Sein Lwin.

Aung Gyi took a more active role, making speeches and writing the government with letters of protest. By the end of July, Sein Lwin had grown irritated with the popular ex-general. When Aung Gyi, and several other former military men who had opposed Ne Win, appeared at a rally at the Shwedagon Pagoda, they were arrested, along with an *Associated Press* reporter covering the event.

By early August, demonstrations erupted almost daily in Rangoon, and they were growing in size and were spreading to other cities. Often as many as 10,000 people gathered at Shwedagon to hear speeches. Many of the people at these rallies carried pictures of Suu's father, Aung San, whose name was quickly becoming a rallying cry.

On August 1, an organization called the All Burma Students' Democratic League called for a nationwide strike, not only by students, but throughout all levels of Burmese society. To help make the strike a success, the students picked an astrologically auspicious date: August 8, 1988, or "8-8-88". In response, the government declared martial law in Rangoon on August 3, again banning public gatherings. But that did not stop the students. Over the next five days rallies continued, and so did the mass arrests and scattered shootings. At their peak, the protests in Rangoon may have included half the adult population of the city. As the unrest spread up the Irrawaddy valley, more army units were brought in, both to quell the protests and to discourage participation in the scheduled "Four Eights" strike.

The Four Eights

At 8 minutes past 8 in the morning of August 8, 1988, Rangoon dockworkers struck, walking off their jobs *en masse*.

About a half-dozen students started marching at the same time the dockworkers struck, carrying their two most popular banners, a red flag embroidered with a bright yellow peacock, and large framed pictures of their revered hero, *Bogyoke* Aung San. "Before long," one of the organizers said, "our column was several thousand long." The crowd steadily grew, picking up people "at every intersection [until] the entire population of Rangoon seemed to be out in the streets."[24] The procession passed the zoo and the defense ministry before converging at City Hall, where they erected makeshift stages for speakers. Other crowds assembled on the lawn of Rangoon General Hospital and in *Bogyoke* Aung San Park. College and high-school students,

Buddhist monks, shopkeepers, manual laborers, house-
wives, all joined in the festivities. Demonstrators even tried
to coax the army soldiers to join in.

The protestor's demanded political and economic reform. Speaker after speaker demanded an end to the failed
"Burmese Way to Socialism," and the end of *Ma Sa La's*
one-party socialist state. Demonstrators searched for Western journalists, eager that stories of the events that had
occurred since March reach the world.

All day long, over 100,000 people marched through
Rangoon. About as many took to the streets in Mandalay,
Burma's second largest city, and Moulmein in the south.
Almost every large city in Burma joined in. Unlike the
protests in late June and early July, these massive uprisings
were mostly peaceful. Though Suu did not join in the
protests of 8-8-88, she seems to have influenced the actions
of the protesters. Apparently her message of non-violence
had taken root among the protesters, for they did little
fighting despite their enormous numbers. In a way, the event
seemed less an imminent uprising than a celebration, a
massive nationwide *pwe*.

Suu Kyi and Bo Thaw address a crowd in 1988.
(Amnesty International)

The Army Starts Shooting

The mass strike and huge protests made the army nervous. If the "Four Eights" strike had been allowed to conclude peacefully, the democratic movement have become unstoppable. Over one million people had participated in the protests—a remarkable number in a country of about forty million. A comparable rally in the United States would be about six million strong, far larger than any protest in U.S. history. The "Four Eights" protesters succeeded in paralyzing the country. What would the emboldened protesters do the next time? The army feared a revolution was coming.

Late in the evening, the army shouted warnings over bullhorns for the crowd to disperse. But the crowd's emotions had gone beyond fear. Buoyed by the portrait of Burma's martyred hero, Aung San, the demonstrators refused to leave. Instead, the mass of people seemed to grow.

The army opened fire into the teeming crowd. No accurate estimate can be made of how many died that night. Men and women, boys and girls, Buddhist monks, students, and workers were gunned down by the soldiers firing indiscriminately into the crowd. Protesters, Western diplomats, and some tourists who happened to be in Rangoon on that day all agree that the army attempted to kill as many people as possible. Some eyewitnesses say the army committed atrocities far beyond gunning down peaceful protesters, and that bodies were thrown into rivers to hide the evidence.

Protests continued for four more days, but the euphoria of the Four Eights was gone. Protesters fought back with *jinglees* to no avail. The army dumped bodies in front of Rangoon General Hospital. Nurses who came forward from the hospital to plead that the killing stop were themselves shot.

Finally, on August 12, Sein Lwin did what may have been the only thing that could have prevented civil war. The hated "Butcher of Burma" resigned. As if by magic, the violence stopped. Perhaps the protesters had won. Some people compared the situation to Czechoslovakia's "Prague Spring" of 1968—a chilling comparison, considering that the Prague uprising had been crushed by Warsaw Pact military forces.

Even if they had finally won, the cost to Burma's protesters had been enormous. A Western diplomat estimated that at least 3,000 people died in those few days of bloodletting.

Dr. Maung Maung replaced Sein Lwin as the head of Burma's government. Maung Maung, a lawyer, newspaper publisher, and historian, had collected an anthology of papers about Aung San, and had written a biography of Ne Win, among other books. Though a civilian, Dr. Maung Maung was a close friend of Ne Win and the army. When he took over for Sein Lwin, Maung Maung promised to hold the referendum on democracy which Ne Win had suggested in July. The protesters, having been disappointed earlier, dismissed his suggestion, saying that the need for a referendum had passed. The people wanted democracy—now.

EIGHT

FATED FOR POLITICS

The tragic Four Eights massacres finally pushed Suu into active politics. Even while what she called the "horrific bloodshed" was continuing, she and an associate named Htwe Myint wrote a letter to the Council of State of Burma, which she released on August 15. Characteristically of Suu, that letter was a very modest declaration. She started by quoting someone *Ma Sa La* could not object to—Ne Win. In his speech on July 23, Ne Win had said:

> I believe the 1988 March and June bloodshed and disturbances were meant. . . to show lack of confidence in Government and the Party behind the Government. . . . Holding a national referendum on what [the people] wish—a one-party system or a multi-party system—would bring out the answer.[25]

Suu threw Ne Win's words back at him: "If we should have to choose between the good of the party and the good of the nation," she quoted, "we should choose the good of the nation."[26]

In effect, Suu said it was time for the Government to choose between party and nation. If Ne Win had spoken truly, solutions to the violence and economic problems would be easy to find.

Suu suggested that *Ma Sa La* convene a "Consultative Committee or some such body," comprised of civil servants, economists, politicians, and other "men of learning and wisdom."[27] The Committee would do nothing but study Burma's problems and suggest solutions.

Suu pleaded that the Government stop shooting demonstrators and release those in prison. Recognizing that both sides had used violence, she also pleaded that the demonstrators remain scrupulously peaceful.

The letter was ignored by the government. Apparently the obscure daughter of Aung San did not warrant their attention at all. But that would quickly change.

A little over a week later, on August 24, Suu appeared at a rally at Rangoon General Hospital. She spoke briefly, announcing her intention to deliver a speech at the Shwedagon pagoda two days later.

By the time Suu announced her planned speech, daily violence had begun again. Mass rallies took place even in smaller towns that had remained quiet during the Four Eights strike. Burma, it seemed, was headed for civil war.

Shwedagon

No one, least of all Suu, expected the reception she got at Shwedagon. The morning after Suu announced she would speak, people began gathering, camping out on the pagoda grounds to make sure they got space up close. By the time she arrived, the crowd was between 500,000 and one million strong. Only a small fraction would actually be able to hear Suu speak. Still they came, excited to see her, as if they expected to see the resurrection of Aung San himself, instead of his daughter. "It is the students who have paved the way" to hold this massive rally, she began. "I therefore request you all to observe a minute's silence ... for those students who have lost their lives."[28]

When the minute had passed she went on, quoting an unimpeachable Burmese hero. "I would like to read to you something my father said about democracy:"

> We must make democracy the popular creed. We must try to build up a free Burma in accordance with such a creed. If we should fail to do this, our people are bound to suffer. .... Democracy is the only ideology which is consistent with freedom. It is also an ideology that promotes and strengthens peace. . . .

"That is what my father said," she continued. "It is the reason why I am participating in this struggle for freedom and democracy in the footsteps and traditions of my father."

The current struggle against despotism was no less important than Aung San's struggle against colonialism forty
years earlier. "This national crisis could in fact be called the
second struggle for national independence."

How was democracy to be achieved? The most important
elements of success, Suu said, were unity and discipline. "If
there is no discipline, no system can succeed. Therefore our
people should always be united and disciplined." Unity,
however, required an almost superhuman capacity to forgive the bloody events from March to August. "Some may
not like what I am going to say. . . . [At] this time there is
a certain amount of dissention between the people and the
army. This rift can lead to future dangers." Not only must
opposition leaders unite; they must also forgive the army
for past events. But unity went further. The army, for its part,
must "become a force in which the people can place their
trust and reliance. May the armed forces become one which
will uphold the honor and dignity of our country." In Suu's
mind, success was inevitable if the entire country would
unite.

Discipline meant not only that the protesters must refrain
from squabbling. They must also refrain from violence. "If
a people. . . can reach their objectives by disciplined and
peaceful means, it would be a most honorable and admirable

achievement." Where should the movement go now, Suu asked? First, all of the students' groups which had arisen over the previous six months should join together. And the time had come, she said, to focus on democracy as the single objective. The protesters must not allow themselves to be distracted by trying to remove hated individuals from the government, nor to be placated with promises of reform referenda. The single goal was democracy. "Our emphatic demands and protests [are] that the one-party system should be dismantled, that a multi-party system of government should be established, and we call for free and fair elections to be arranged as quickly as possible. These are our demands," she concluded.

If *Maung* Phone Maw's death in March was the spark which ignited the wildfire of protest that had raged throughout Burma, Aung San Suu Kyi's speech at the Shwedagon pagoda added fuel to the fire, collected its power and aimed it along a constructive path. Though Suu had jumped headlong into the conflagration, she remained a reluctant politician. In an interview a few days after the Shwedagon speech, she was asked what her goals were. She answered, "I am one of a large majority of people in Burma struggling for democracy. It is my aim to help the people attain democracy without further violence or loss of life."[29] Asked what role she would take in the struggle, she said, "There is no particular role in which I see myself. I shall wait on events to see how I can be of most use." Finally, she described herself as little more than a convenient tool. "A life in politics holds no attraction for me. At the moment I serve as a kind of unifying force because of my father's name."

Suu frequently used the image of herself as "my father's daughter."[30] In a very real way she saw her duty during Burma's strife as a continuation of Aung San's work. "I don't pretend that I don't owe my position in Burmese politics to my father. . . . I'm doing this for my father. I'm quite happy that they see me as my father's daughter. My only concern is that I prove worthy of him."[31]

Perhaps emboldened by the enormous response to Suu's speech, U Tin U, a former army general who had been jailed by Ne Win for four years, joined her in calling for unity and peace the day after Suu's Shwedagon speech. The next day U Nu announced the formation of a new political party, the League for Democracy and Peace. Along with Aung Gyi, the letter writer who had unexpectedly been released from prison the day before Suu's speech, these men and Suu formed the nucleus around which the democracy movement soon revolved. But both Aung Gyi and Tin U were somewhat suspect, for though they had both been persecuted by Ne Win, they had served in his government before losing

Suu Kyi with U Tin U, as leaders of the National League for Democracy, in 1989. (Amnesty International)

his favor. Another problem was that *U* Nu, whose democratic credentials were second only to Aung San himself, was over eighty years old. Almost by default, that left Suu to take charge. In spite of her distaste for politics, Suu pressed on. The house on University Avenue became headquarters to her increasing band of followers, where they planned a sustained, carefully directed program of civil disobedience.

In late August some political prisoners, and thousands of convicted criminals, "escaped" from jails throughout the country. Opponents of the government claimed that the criminals were intentionally set free by the government in order to convince the average citizen that the protests had created social chaos. As the criminals took to the streets unrest was no longer limited to political protest. General lawlessness was growing rapidly. The police seemed unable to control rioters and looters. More ominously, the authorities seemed unwilling to control them. Critics of the government suspected that it was creating an excuse for a new crackdown.

Temporarily freed from the army's intimidation, protesters grew bolder, and sometimes degenerated into mere mobs, or turned into vigilante gangs. Protesters began holding mock trials of *Lon Htein* "spies" who had infiltrated the students' organizations. In several dozen of these ugly incidents, "convicted spies" were summarily executed. When Suu heard of an impending mock trial, she and her followers rushed to halt the execution, pleading that the students stay above such hatred. Some of the students' fiercest violence was directed at people who had attacked Suu by distributing leaflets that contained crude drawings, and called her obscene names. Despite these personal attacks, Suu insisted that the violence stop. Such tactics could never help their cause.

In spite of such incidents, most of the protests remained peaceful, and Suu's message of non-violence gained support. An incident that took place near the U.S. Embassy in August is typical. A crowd and the army confronted each other in the street. The army threatened to shoot if the crowd did not disperse. A young boy, perhaps just old enough to be entering high school, emerged from the crowd, and walked toward the soldiers. Alone in the street, the boy ripped open his shirt. He stood still, arms held wide, presenting his bare chest as a target for the soldiers' weapons. It was a wordless challenge: shoot or stand aside. But it was not an empty gesture. No one doubted the soldiers could have fired into the crowd; it had happened often before. But the sight of such a young boy offering his life was too much even for soldiers used to killing. Not a shot was fired. The army yielded, and the protest went on.

By early September, the whole of Burma had almost ceased functioning. The students launched a new, crippling strike. Protesters and criminals ran free in the streets. Foreign embassies began evacuating diplomats' families. Stephen Solarz, a visiting U.S. Congressman, left Burma convinced that *Ma Sa La's* government could not count on the army's loyalty, and that civil war was imminent. In such a war, Solarz said, America's support should be with the protesters. This was the first suggestion that U.S. aid for Burma's war on opium growers should end.

On September 9, *U* Nu stunned everyone, especially Suu and the leaders of the League for Democracy and Peace. He announced that, as he had been Prime Minister when Ne Win seized power, he was now the legitimate leader of Burma. He announced that he would call for new elections soon.

U Nu's announcement ended his role as a credible opposition leader. No one took him seriously any longer. *Ma Sa La* ignored him. In an interview with the BBC the next day, *U* Nu belittled the importance of the other leaders, such as Suu and Aung Gyi. Asked if he had consulted them, *U* Nu said, "Why do you think that we need to consult with them? You give me the answer. . . . They can do what they want, I will not object and I will do what I want."[32] It seemed that Burma's long history of political feuding by "thin skinned" politicians might break up the unity Suu sought. Aung Gyi and Suu quickly issued a statement saying they thought *U* Nu's declaration was impractical, and that the Burmese people must construct their new government. The next day, *U* Nu's "government" collapsed.

Restoration of Law and Order

By mid-September, 1988, Burma was in a state of anarchy. The rumors accusing *Ma Sa La* of purposefully allowing the disorder to continue, which had earlier been dismissed as too outrageous to believe, now seemed true. General Saw Maung, the head of the army, had served under Ne Win in the Fourth Burma Rifles, and was as loyal to "The Old Man" as a son is to a respected father. On September 19, Saw Maung staged a military *coup d'etat*. Outside commentators asked the obvious question: how could the army, already in functional control of the government, stage a "coup"? Nevertheless, Maung Maung's government was ousted and *Ma Sa La's* reign over Burma was ended. *Ma Sa La*, the Burmese Socialist Program Party, disbanded and regrouped as the National Union Party (NUP). But the NUP was merely a front group. After the coup, the army ruled directly. Saw Maung immediately formed the State Law and Order Restoration Council (SLORC) to rule Burma.

Once again, the protesters felt the brutal hand of the army. People were killed indiscriminately and their dead bodies loaded uncounted into trucks to be carted away. But now the world was watching Burma. Japan, which had earlier suspended aid, condemned the military's actions. The United States waited to see SLORC's solution to the anarchy. They did not have to wait long. The army fired into a crowd right in front of the U.S. Embassy, killing several people. On a videotape recovered after the shooting, a reporter and cameraman's last words are recorded: "What shall we do?" the cameraman asked. His companion responded, "Keep on filming until they shoot at us."[33]

Within a week of the military takeover all U.S. aid was canceled to protest SLORC's brutality. On September 27, the European Community condemned SLORC and called for the killings to stop.

But the killing continued. Many of the dead were high-school students. Within a week the violence had broken the back of the protest movement. Estimates of the dead ran from the government's dubious official number of 263, to other estimates as high as 10,000. To escape the military, students and other protesters began fleeing to the Thailand border, and the violence subsided.

Suu's initial reaction to the takeover by SLORC is recorded in several letters she sent to Amnesty International, an international organization devoted to recording and ending the human rights abuses committed by governments against their own people. The letter urged the group to lobby diplomats at the United Nations to intervene in Burma's crisis. She stressed that large numbers of children and Buddhist monks were being slaughtered in the streets. Though in the letters she does not say exactly what she would like the UN to do, it is clear from her other statements that she felt the slaughter could not continue if the supply of weapons that flowed into Burma from other counties were cut off.

Suu now totally abandoned her anti-political stance. After Ne Win's speech on July 23, she had hoped that he would yield Burma's political power to the people. But power had been passed only to a new generation of military dictators. She realized SLORC could maintain dictatorial rule into future generations.

SLORC had said its only purpose was to "restore law and order." After that was done, elections would be allowed. It legalized multiple political parties. Suu, Aung Gyi, and Tin U decided to take the military at its word. On September 24, the day after the U.S. cut off aid, the three opposition leaders formed the National League for Democracy (NLD).

They intensified their call for an end to undisciplined mass protests. All the protesters' energies should be directed toward two goals: bringing Burma's plight to the world community so that SLORC could not refuse to hold elections, and winning the elections when they occurred. Protests should be dedicated to furthering these two goals. If SLORC refused to let them meet, or to publish pamphlets, they must do so anyway.

From September through December, the National League for Democracy spread its message, and membership grew. The NLD quickly overtook the pro-SLORC National Union Party as Burma's largest political party. Suu travelled the country, giving speeches and winning converts. She also continued to spread the message throughout the world. She sent more letters to Amnesty International, publicizing the military's brutality. Although persecution of the protesters continued, few were now being shot in the streets. Students were being rounded up to be worked as human mules carrying supplies to the soldiers fighting in the government's forty-year-old wars with insurgents along the borders. Large groups of students were seen stripped naked and corralled like animals, waiting to be sent to the fronts. Worse, it was widely reported that arrested students were being forced to walk across minefields. They were being used as human minesweepers.

Raising the Heat

However deeply involved Suu became in Burmese politics, her first duty as 1988 ended was still to her mother's health. Despite Suu's care, Khin Kyi continued to deteriorate. On December 27, 1988, she died, at the age of 75.

Daw Khin Kyi's funeral on January 2, 1989 marked the next turning point in Burma's democracy movement. About 100,000 people lined the streets of Rangoon for the funeral procession. Suu pleaded with the crowd to be "calm and disciplined in sending my mother on her last journey."[34] It is a measure of the respect Burma paid to *Daw* Khin Kyi, as well an indication of how Suu's support had grown, that the day passed without violence. Even General Saw Maung, the head of SLORC, came to pay his respects.

That day seemed to set the tone for 1989. From then on Suu's support grew, and she, freed from concerns about her mother, turned up the heat on the military government. She travelled farther, and for longer periods. Occasionally, she spoke to as many as a dozen villages in a single day. Though she spoke to the international community in English, she talked to the Burmese people in fluent Burmese. Little of what she said has been translated into English, but it is clear that her message remained constant: discipline and unity among the people would bring peaceful progress toward democracy.

In February 1989, SLORC announced that elections would be held in the spring of 1990, although they did not set an exact date. Suu intended to use the year before the elections to build the NLD's reputation. Daily she gave speeches. Her rallies took on a very disciplined, controlled air. She missed few opportunities to draw support away from SLORC and their political supporters in the National Union Party. On every national holiday, the NLD refused to participate in the official celebrations, preferring to hold their own. These events became an informal way of polling the people to see which party they supported.

Daw Khin Kyi's funeral overshadowed the celebration of Burmese independence day on January 4. Several foreign diplomats who attended the funeral showed their support for the opposition to military government by flying to Thailand immediately after the funeral to avoid attending the official independence day celebration. On Armed Forces Day, the anniversary of Aung San's March 27 attack on the Japanese during World War II, NLD events drew people away from the government's official celebrations. The NLD also took advantage of the upcoming anniversaries of the slaughters of 1988. On March 13, Phone Maw's death was commemorated, followed quickly by the anniversary of the White Bridge killings.

Gradually, clashes between the NLD and the government grew more heated. At first, Suu talked to small groups indoors, but eventually, as the crowds grew larger, the rallies had to be moved outdoors. This made confrontation with the army inevitable. In June, she was briefly arrested while commemorating a killing of the previous year. In Rangoon, Suu was constantly followed by army trucks telling people not to listen to her, and blaring music and noise to drown out what she said. In the countryside, the army went further. They physically harassed Suu and her NLD companions, raised barbed-wire fences to keep people away from her speeches, and arrested her followers.

Suu responded by demanding the firings of army officers who ordered the harassment. But the army continued its campaign of fear and intimidation. Sometimes the army blocked Suu's way, and at other times it made physical threats. In the most serious incident, the army ordered a group of marchers to disband, threatening to shoot if they did not. Suu, unarmed, left the others behind and walked alone toward the soldiers. An officer ordered a group of six soldiers to prepare to shoot. Guns were levelled at her. Another warning followed, but Suu never flinched. Before the order to shoot was given, a more senior officer ordered the soldiers to lower their guns. The army fell back and allowed the march to continue. Later, SLORC said the proper action by the army would have been to fire on Suu and the crowd behind her, and it was reported that the officer who rescinded the order to shoot was demoted.

SLORC fought back against Suu and the National League for Democracy in two ways. First, it attacked Suu personally, claiming that her marriage to a foreigner, and her long residence outside Burma, made her patriotism suspect. Ne Win and *Ma Sa La* had for a long time taken advantage of animosities that had lingered since colonial days, between the Burmese and immigrants, mainly Indians, Chinese, and Westerners, blaming the failures of the "Burmese Way to Socialism" on them. Now they tried to brand Suu as one of the foreigners they blamed for Burma's problems.

Then, as Suu had predicted, SLORC tried to label the NLD a "communist" conspiracy. In the late 1980's the Communist Party of Burma was finally losing the civil war it had waged since the 1940's. A few disillusioned communists joined the National League for Democracy. The NLD, whose main requirement was a commitment to work peacefully for democracy, welcomed these members. SLORC immediately branded the entire group a communist organization. Aung Gyi, who joined the military in accusing the NLD of being dominated by the communists, split with Suu and Tin U, and left the NLD.

Though the government had pledged "free and fair"

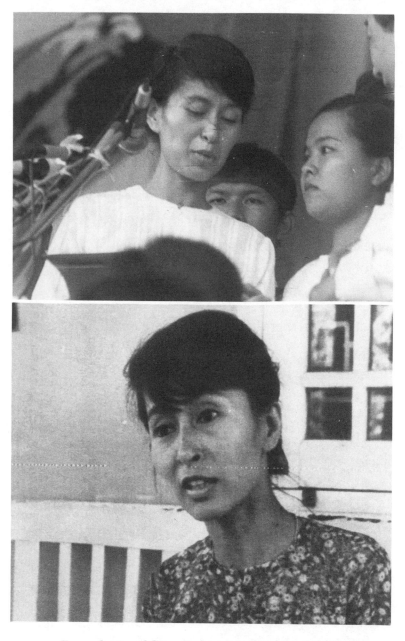

*Two shots of Suu Kyi campaigning during
the 1989 elections.* (Agence France Presse)

elections, its actions belied the promise. No party but the National Union Party was allowed to meet or to publish papers. Its members spread ugly rumors about Suu, and distributed posters showing drawings of her which one reporter described as "startlingly obscene."[35]

As of March 1989, although the NLD was still a legal party, it was not allowed to print or distribute pamphlets detailing its philosophy. In response, its members came up with novel ways to get their message out. They sought out foreign journalists, especially those whose reports were made available to the British Broadcasting Corporation and the Voice of America, organizations that broadcast news into Burma by shortwave radio. Suu's speeches were also recorded on videotape and circulated secretly. In some places, Suu's videos were more popular than those of the most popular American rock groups, which are also outlawed in Burma. People starved for news were willing to pay a week's wages for a Suu video. Suu's jacket and *lungyi,* and the NLD's peasant's hat symbol, became Burma's popular fashion statement. The American Ambassador even compared the Burmese excited response to Suu to that of a teenager meeting a rock star.

In May, Suu turned up the heat again. She started using Ne Win's name in her speeches, a practice unheard of in over two decades—he was usually called "The Old Man" or

"Number One". In spite of all the official changes in leadership, many Burmese still believed that Ne Win called the shots. Suu began laying the blame for Burma's troubles directly on Ne Win. More importantly, she started talking about her father's opinions of Ne Win, who was one of Burma's "Thirty Heroes." For his entire reign, Ne Win had claimed to be carrying on the work of Aung San. But Suu shattered his claim to Aung San's legacy. Ne Win, Suu said, was one of the men Aung San least liked in the army. He objected to Ne Win because of his fiery temper, lax morals, and weakness for worldly pleasures, when there was so much work to be done.

Throughout June, SLORC grew more and more concerned about the National League for Democracy's verbal assaults. They realized that if things continued as they were going, the pro-SLORC National Union Party would lose a free and fair election. Even more troubling to the military was an incident during Suu's latest trip to the countryside. Several army units not only stopped harassing her, but threw flowers at her and had joined the very crowd they were supposed to be dispersing. With Martyrs' Day, the July 19 commemoration of Aung San's assassination, coming quickly, and so soon after that the anniversaries of Ne Win's resignation and the "Four Eights," the government might not even survive until the promised 1990 elections.

NINE

UNDER ARREST

Aung San is buried near the grounds of the Shwedagon pagoda. Only eleven months earlier, when she entered the political struggle, Suu had drawn a crowd of half a million to the pagoda, with just two days advance notice. She had grown much more popular in the months since her Shwedagon speech. How many people might now come to hear her honor her martyred father, who was also the rallying symbol for the new democracy movement? Suu's speech could spark a revolution. Some reporters compared the situation in Burma to that of the Philippines in 1987, where a mass uprising forced dictator Ferdinand Marcos into exile. They also compared Suu to Corazon Aquino, the widow of Marcos's assassinated political rival, Benigno Aquino, who became President of the Philippines after Marcos had fled the country. Suu dismissed the comparison as highly inaccurate.

The government feared Martyr's Day, and what could follow a successful speech by Suu, more than anything else, including world opinion. Suu could hardly be allowed to lead a rally at her father's grave. They announced that no Martyr's Day rally would be allowed. It was also announced that political prisoners would face one of three punishments: death, life in prison, or three years at hard labor. Mass arrests of NLD members began. Foreign journalists were rounded up and deported to Thailand, after being given the horrifying explanation that the government did not want them to see what would transpire over the next few days. On July 17, two days before the anniversary, the army flooded into Rangoon and Mandalay. Telephone and telex lines into Burma were cut. Reporters in Bangkok, Thailand began warning the world to expect a new round of killing in Burma.

Rather than submit her followers to almost certain slaughter, Suu canceled the rally. By forcing the government to expose its brutality even before Martyr's Day began, she had already scored a victory. She spent the day quietly in her house on University Avenue.

The next morning, July 20, when Suu tried to go to Shwedagon pagoda to place flowers on her father's grave, she was met by armed guards, who refused to let her leave.

She was arrested and confined to her house. Her sons, Alexander and Kim, were there with her. Michael Aris, in Scotland for the funeral of his own father, flew to Rangoon to be with his wife.

The first few weeks of Suu's detention were chaotic. The authorities in Rangoon had allowed Michael to join Suu, but would not allow the British Embassy to talk with him, which created a furor in Britain. On the evening after her arrest, Suu started a hunger strike, demanding humane treatment of the many arrested NLD members. The news of Suu's hunger strike was published in *Time* magazine, bringing even greater publicity to the arrest. Over the next two weeks, Suu's health declined. On August 1, after the government promised there would be no mistreatment of her followers, Suu finally ended her fast. Two weeks later, the British Consul was allowed to meet with Michael.

After Suu recovered from her hunger strike, Michael and the boys made plans to return to England. The boys needed to return to school, and Michael had obligations at Oxford. Burmese authorities agreed to allow mail to be delivered to the house, and to let Suu write her family. In early September, Suu's husband and sons boarded an airplane for home. None of them knew it would be years before they would all be together again.

After the arrest of Suu and her fellow NLD leaders, Burma had settled into a tense stalemate. Election preparations went forward. In February, 1990, SLORC announced new restrictions on political campaigning. It was not about to let a new popular leader rise up to take Suu's place.

On May 27, 1990, Burma held its first "democratic" election since that of *U* Nu in 1960. No one expected the event to be "free and fair." Though multiple parties were allowed to participate, SLORC obviously intended for their National Union Party to dominate the election. Most candidates with broad, nationwide appeal, like Suu and Tin U, were disqualified, and their names were removed from the ballot. Suu and Tin U themselves remained prisoner's. Apparently the military leadership thought its intimidation during the campaign would ensure the results it wanted, for there was little effort made to stuff the ballot boxes. The western journalists allowed to observe the voting announced that the balloting was "free and fair." Nevertheless, because of the repression that took place before voting began, the international community dismissed the election before it occurred.

The election results were stunning—especially to SLORC. In almost every district, Suu's National League for Democracy won large victories. Many people voted for the NLD without even knowing who their local candidate was. They cared only that it was Suu's party. When all the ballots had been counted, the NLD won nearly two-thirds of the popular vote, and over 80% of the seats in the new legislature.

After losing the election, SLORC simply changed the rules. It declared that the vote had not, after all, been held to elect a new government, but merely to elect representatives to a constituent assembly whose task was to write a new constitution. Then it refused to allow the assembly to meet. In effect, SLORC said it would not allow the elected assembly to meet until after the framework of a new constitution had been negotiated, an impossible restriction. They had decided that the election meant nothing.

For two months after the vote, unrest subsided while protesters waited to see if the military would turn over power. In July, Suu's detention was extended for another year. By August, unrest was again building. On August 8, the second anniversary of the "Four Eights" rally, Buddhist monks led a rally in Mandalay. A diplomat reported that at least two monks and two students were killed by troops. A few days later, the human rights group Asia Watch reported that arrests were continuing, that "torture, including electric shocks, beatings, sleep deprivation and cigarette burns, is widespread," and that 100 death sentences had been passed for political protesters.[36] By September, reports were com-

Michael Aris with Suu Kyi in front of her
family home on University Avenue in Ragoon.
(Sygma/Dominique Aubert)

ing from Rangoon that Burmese soldiers were going onto the grounds of the American, German, British, and other embassies looking for dissidents seeking political refuge, a clear violation of international law. The army also raided Buddhist monasteries looking for protesters.

By the end of 1990, the open expression of democratic demands in Burma was effectively forbidden. In a last, symbolic move, Dr. Sein Win, Suu's cousin and one of the few NLD leaders not yet in prison, fled to the Thai border and proclaimed a rival government-in-exile.

Since 1990, almost every nation has condemned Burma for its human rights abuses. With all foreign aid cut off, SLORC has sold off much of Burma's natural resources to pay for its military needs. The teak forests have been decimated by companies from Thailand. Large oil exploration concessions have been sold to many Western oil companies. The economy, however, shows few signs of improving, and, as in the days of British colonial rule, little of the money from these sales is ever seen by the average Burmese.

International pressure increased during 1991. Through Suu, the plight of the dissidents stayed in the international spotlight. Near the end of 1990, Norway awarded her that year's Thorolf Rafto Prize for Human Rights. The following July, the European Parliament awarded her the 1991 Sakharov Prize for Freedom of Thought, an award named after the late Russian dissident Andrei Sakharov. Finally, on October 14, 1991, the Norwegian Nobel Committee announced it had selected Suu as the winner of the 1991 Peace Prize. Previous Nobel Laureates joined in a call demanding freedom for Suu and other Burmese political prisoners. All the prize money from these awards, including the $1.2 million which came with the Nobel Prize, was put into a trust fund by Suu for the health and education of the Burmese people.

Since 1991, Suu's family has managed to keep her plight—and Burma's plight—in the world's consciousness, despite the fact that she is held in almost total isolation.

From the start, Suu has refused any aid from her captors. She even insisted on paying for all the food brought into the house. The few times Michael Aris has been allowed to see her since 1989, he has had to bring suitcases packed with food to help support her. The only people she is allowed to see on a regular basis are a young girl who comes in to help with the housework, and a military officer who acts as a spokesman for the government.

After her sons left Rangoon in September 1989, the government canceled their passports, making it difficultt for them to return. Finally, in 1992, they were allowed in for a short visit on British passports. Since then, Suu's family has been allowed to visit her several times, the latest of which was at Christmas in 1993.

Suu's life under house arrest has settled into a patient routine. She rises early. To help maintain her health, as well as her spirits, she maintains a rigorous daily schedule. Every day she exercises, then studies both the literature she loves and Buddhist scriptures. For several years she played her piano daily, but this stopped in 1991. Many people specu-lated that she had sold the piano for food, but after Michael was allowed to visit her in 1992, he supplied the real reason: though she had sold other furniture for food, she had practically worn the piano out. So many strings and keys had broken that she could play only simple tunes on it.

Michael Aris has been able to bring out of Burma new speeches Suu has written, or English translations of her older speeches. Her sons have presented these before gatherings on several occasions. When the International Human Rights Law Group honored Suu with an award in May 1992, Alexander Aris read her acceptance speech. It read in part: "I have always in mind all the people of my country who have struggled so hard to establish their right to shape their national destiny. It is in their name and in the name of my colleagues that I accept this award with sincere thanks."[37] Just a month later, on June 13, 1992, Alexander again spoke for his mother at the opening ceremonies of the Summer Olympic Games in Barcelona, Spain. In 1993, Alexander and his brother Kim read her speeches to meetings of Poets, Essayists, and Novelists (PEN) International.

In 1991, Michael Aris collected Suu's writings and published them as *Freedom From Fear*, the title of an essay Suu had written some time earlier. That essay, first printed after the European Parliament's award of the Sakharov Prize, summed up Suu's philosophy on Burma's plight. "It is not power that corrupts," Suu wrote, "but fear."

> Fear of losing power corrupts those who wield it
> and fear of the scourge of power corrupts those
> who are subject to it. . . . Public dissatisfaction
> with economic hardships has been seen as the
> chief cause of the movement for democracy in
> Burma. . . . But it was more than the difficulties
> of eking out a barely acceptable standard of
> living that had eroded the patience of a
> traditionally good-natured, quiescent people—it
> was also the humiliation of a way of life disfigured
> by corruption and fear.[38]

It is this fear Suu seeks to end. She finished by quoting Mahatma Gandhi: "The greatest gift for an individual or a nation. . . was. . . fearlessness, not merely bodily courage but absence of fear from the mind."[39]

TEN

A RESOLUTION
WITHOUT AN END

As of this writing, Aung San Suu Kyi remains imprisoned in her home on University Avenue along Rangoon's Inya Lake. In February 1994, four and one half years after Suu was arrested, the military government of Burma eased their policy of enforced isolation slightly. The guards surrounding her house were removed, and on February 14, U.S. Representative Bill Richardson, along with a United Nations observer and a reporter from the *New York Times*, were allowed to meet with Suu in her house. Except for her husband and sons, these were her first visitors since her arrest in 1989.

After meeting with Suu for more than five hours stretched over a two day period, Richardson reported that Suu remains unwavering in her determination to see democracy come to

Burma. He expressed optimism that negotiations would begin soon. The *New York Times* reporter, Philip Shenon, speculated that the economic isolation Burma has endured because of its treatment of Suu and other human rights abuses, may finally be forcing the military government to consider serious reform.

Ironically, across the lake, perhaps within Suu's sight, lives Ne Win, the man many people blame for Suu's arrest. Like Suu, Ne Win is, in a way, also imprisoned in his own home. He fears for his life if he should be seen in public. Some people say he has his food tested for poison. One of his daughters carries a gun at all times.

Aung San Suu Kyi has said that the time has not yet come to write her life story, for the resolution is not yet known. Perhaps she is right. She has lived her whole life with a strong feeling of duty toward Burma, but she has also lived most of it as a quiet, retiring person. Biographers searching for facts on her early life have a difficult job. She was not originally an activist. She was not controversial. She was not ambitious. Even when she began appearing in public, she played down her own personality while emphasizing her ideas.

Before returning to Burma to nurse her dying mother, Suu was content to remain quietly out of the public eye content not in a complacent, carefree sense, but in the Buddhist sense. Buddhism requires patience. Suu was and is content in the knowledge that Burma's long sufferings must someday end. She will accept whatever role she must perform in bringing that goal about. If things had gone as Suu hoped, Ne Win would have peacefully relinquished power, and she would have returned to help rebuild Burma, starting with the children.

But Suu's life did not turn out that way. Her mother's illness immersed her in Burma's first real opportunity for reform in a quarter century. She brought to that opportunity a sense of purpose and a strong, steady leadership. When it seemed the democracy movement might succeed, its leaders were arrested. Now Suu lives, as she has for over five years, isolated even from her own family. She could have it differently: Burma's rulers have repeatedly offered her the option of exile. She could leave Burma and return to her Oxford life. But she refuses to turn her back on her country.

No one knows what will happen to Aung San Suu Kyi. She may emerge from detention to lead Burma back to democracy. Though it seems very unlikely, she may tire of the battle and return to the comfortable life she abandoned in 1988. She may die in detention.

But in a greater sense, it does not matter which of the possible endings comes to pass. We have a resolution, though we do not yet know the end. Suu has written her own resolution:

> It's not by living to the age of ninety or one hundred that one lives the full life. Some people live well until they are ninety or one hundred without ever having done anything for anyone. They come into the world, live, then die without doing something for the world. I don't think that this is living a full life. To live the full life one must have the courage to bear the responsibility of the needs of others—one must want to bear this responsibility. Each and every one of us must have this attitude and we must instill it in our youth.[40]

Regardless of what is to come, *Daw* Aung San Suu Kyi has instilled that courage in her own sons, and in the sons and daughters of Burma. Aung San Suu Kyi has indeed lived the full life.

CHRONOLOGY FOR BURMA (MYANMAR)

1044-1287	First Unification. King Anawrahta unites Burmese ethnic groups; strongly promotes Theravada Buddhism.
1287	Pagan sacked by Mongols; Burmese kingdom splits.
1486-c.1729	Second Unification; King Minkyinyo reunites Burma.
c.1498	First contact between Burma and Westerners (Portuguese).
c.1600	First contact with British.
c.1600-c.1760	British East India Company conquers India.
1729-55	Mons rebel against Burman rulers.
c.1752	Third Unification; King Alaungpaya conquers Mons.

c.1795-1824	Border dispute with India.
1824	First Burmese-British war; southern (Tenasserim) and northern (Arakan) coastal regions under British rule.
1852	Second Burmese-British war; British control extends to central Burmese coast and Irrawaddy River valley.
1852	Mindon overthrows King Pagan, his brother.
1878	King Mindon dies. Thibaw takes throne.
1885	Third Burmese-British war; British rule all Burma, which becomes an administrative state of India.
1886-90	Pacification of anti-British guerilla warfare.
1905	Japanese victory in Russo-Japanese war.
1920's	Burmese Nationalism increases.
1920-2	Rangoon University students strike; unrest spreads nationwide. National school movement.
1923	Dyarchy constitution takes effect.
1930's	Worldwide economic distress affects Burma.

1930-1	Saya San rebellion.
1931	Burma Round Table in London reviews Dyarchy.
1936	Students at Rangoon University and elsewhere protest against British rule.
1937	New constitution separates British Burma from India.
1941	Japanese oust the British from Burma.
1942-5	Japanese occupy Burma.
1945	Aung San aids British in reoccupying Burma; negotiations for independence begin.
19 July 1947	Aung San and others in government assassinated.
4 Jan. 1948	Burma granted independence from Great Britain.
2 Mar. 1962	Ne Win assumes dictatorial powers in military coup.
7 July 1962	Students protest takeover. Student Union demolished.
13 Mar. 1988	Student/military clash starts five days of protests.
9 May 1988	Government report dramatically underestimating casualties of March 13-18 triggers months of protests.

23 July 1988	Ne Win steps down.
8 Aug. 1988	8-8-88 protests start; 3000 die over three days.
18 Sep. 1988	General Saw Maung stages military "takeover".
27 May 1990	NLD wins elections but is denied the right to form a civilian government.

CHRONOLOGY FOR
AUNG SAN SUU KYI

19 June 1945	Born in Rangoon, Burma to Aung San and Khin Kyi.
19 July 1947	Aung San assassinated.
c.1953	Brother, age 9, dies in drowning accident.
1960	*Daw* Khin Kyi appointed Burmese Ambassador to India.
1964-1967	Undergraduate at St Hugh's College, Oxford.
1967	*Daw* Khin Kyi retires to estate in Rangoon.
1967-1969	Teaching and historical research.
1969 - 1971	Studies at New York University. UN employee.
1972	Marries Michael Aris, moves to Bhutan.

1973	Moves to London. Alexander Aris (son) born.
1976	Aris and Aung San Suu Kyi settle in Oxford.
1977	Kim Aris (son) born.
1984	Publishes *Aung San*, biography of her father.
1985	Publishes *Let's Visit Burma*, a history.
1985 - 1986	Scholarship to University of Kyoto.
1987	Fellow at Institute of Advanced Studies, in New Delhi.
1987	Publishes "Socio-Political Currents in Burmese Literature, 1910-1940" in *Burma and Japan*
1988	Student at London University's School of Oriental and African Studies.
Mar-Apr. 1988	*Daw* Khin Kyi suffers stroke; Aung San Suu Kyi returns to Rangoon to tend to ailing mother.
24 Aug. 1988	At Rangoon General Hospital, announces her intention to deliver an address at Shwedagon.
26 Aug. 1988	Delivers first major speech at the Shwedagon Pagoda.

24 Sep. 1988	Organizes NLD with Aung Gyi and Tin U.
28 Sep. 1988	Appointed Secretary General of National League for Democracy (NLD).
27 Dec. 1988	*Daw* Khin Kyi dies.
20 July 1989	Placed under house arrest at her estate in Rangoon; many followers arrested.
July-Aug 1989	Hunger strike, demanding humane treatment of her arrested followers.
22 Dec. 1989	Agrees to stand for election.
1990	Wins Rafto Award.
27 May 1990	NLD wins landslide election victory.
July 1991	Wins 1990 Sakharov Prize for Freedom of Thought.
14 Oct. 1991	Wins Nobel Peace Prize.
10 Dec. 1991	Alexander and Kim Aris accept Nobel for Aung San Suu Kyi.
May 1992	Allowed visit from family at house in Rangoon.
20 Jul. 1993	House arrest extended for another year.
14 Feb. 1994	Meets with U.S. and U.N. delegation.

BIBLIOGRAPHY

Aung San Suu Kyi (Michael Aris, ed.), *Freedom From Fear and Other Writings* (New York: Penguin, 1991)

Aung San Suu Kyi, "Aung San" and "My Country, My People," in *Freedom From Fear* (New York: Penguin, 1991)

Kelen, Betty, *Gautama Buddha in Life and Legend* (New York: Lothrop, Lee and Shepard Co, 1967)

Maung Htin Aung, *A History of Burma* (New York: Colombia University Press, 1967)

Shway Yoe, *The Burman* (New York: W. W. Norton, 1963)

Also used in the preparation of this volume:

Books:

Aung San, (Josef Silverstein, ed.), *The Political Legacy of Aung San* (Ithaca, New York: Cornell University, 1972)

Cady, John Frank, *A History of Modern Burma* (Ithaca, New York: Cornell University Press, 1958)

Kanbawza Win, Daw *Aung San Suu Kyi, The Nobel Laureate: A Burmese Perspective* (Bangkok: CPDSK Publications, 1993)

Lintner, Bertil, *Aung San Suu Kyi and the Unfinished Burmese Renaissance* (Clayton, Australia: The Centre of Southeast Asian Studies, 1990)

-------, *Outrage: Burma's Struggle for Democracy* (London: White Lotus, 1990)

Maung Maung, ed., *Aung San of Burma* (The Hague: Martinus Nyhoff, 1962)

Maung Maung Gyi, *Burmese Political Values: The Socio-political Roots of Authoritarianism* (New York: Praeger, 1983)

Mya Maung, *Totalitarianism in Burma: Prospects for Economic Development* (New York: Paragon House, 1992)

Steinberg, David I., *The Future of Burma: Crisis and Choice in Myanmar* (Lanham, Maryland: University Press of America, 1990)

Trager, Frank N., *Burma: From Kingdom to Republic; A Historical and Political Analysis* (New York: Frederick A. Praeger, 1966)

Periodicals:

Asian Survey
The Christian Science Monitor
Congressional Record
Current Biography
The Economist (London)
The Far Eastern Economic Review
Indian Express (Bombay)
The New York Times
Time Magazine
The Times (London)
The Washington Post

GLOSSARY

Bo — General.

Bogyoke — Great General.

Chinlon — A game similar to hacky-sac.

Daw — Literally "Aunt." A title used in Burmese as "Mrs" is used in English. Compare to *Ma* below.

Dobama Asiayone — The We Burmese Society, formed in 1935 to work for independence from Great Britain.

Gonnyinto — A game similar to penny-pitching.

Hluttaw — The advisory council to the King in pre-British Burma.

Jinglee — A homemade slingshot which fires sharpened bicycle spokes.

Lanzins — See *Myanma Sosialit Lanzin Pati*

Lon Htein — Riot Police.

Lungyi — A long, wrap-around skirt similar to the Japanese sarong.

Ma — Literally "Sister." A title used in Burmese as "Miss" is used in English. Compare to *Daw* above.

Ma Sa La — See *Myanma Sosialit Lanzin Pati*

Maung — Literally "Brother." A title used in Burmese as "Master" is used in English. Compare to *U* below. Maung is also a common name in Burma.

Min — King; Government.

Minlawn — Pretender to the throne.

Myanma Sosialit Lanzin Pati — Burma Socialist Program Party.

Myothugyi — Hereditary village official in pre-British Burma.

Nat — A spirit of the earth.

Nirvana — The perfected state Buddhists strive for, which signifies the cessation of earthly pain and suffering.

Pwe — Literally "play," but actually any large festival.

Sangha — The Buddhist clergy.

Thakin — Literally "Master". The title assumed by members of the *Dobama Asiayone*.

U — Literally "Uncle." A title used in Burmese as "Mr" is used in English. U is also a common name in Burma. Compare to *Maung* above. In this volume, the titles *U* and *Maung* are printed in italics to differentiate them from the names U and Maung.

NOTES

Chapter One
The Guest Of Honor Can't Be Here

[1] Aris, Alexander, Nobel Peace Prize Acceptance Speech, 10 December 1991.

[2] *Ibid.*

Chapter Two
The Kingdom Of Burma

[3] Cady, John F., *A History of Modern Burma* (Ithica, New York: Cornell University Press, 1958), p. 613.

[4] *Maung* Maung Gyi, *Burmese Political Values: The Socio-political Roots of Authoritarianism* (New York: Praeger, 1983), p. 47.

[5] Steinberg, David I., *The Future of Burma: Crisis and Choice in Myanmar* (Lanham, Maryland: University Press of America, 1990), p. 1. See also Cady, p. 368.

Chapter Three
Colonial Burma

[6] Trager, Frank N., *Burma: From Kingdom to Republic; A Historical and Political Analysis* (New York: Frederick A. Praeger, 1966), p. 22.

[7] Cady, pp. 132-3.

[8] Trager, pp. 37-8.

[9] Cady, p. 108.

[10] Htin Aung, *A History of Burma* (New York: Colombia University Press, 1967), p. 203.

[11] *Ibid.*, p. 269.

[12] *Ibid.*, p. 269.
Chapter Four
Aung San's Legacy

[13] Aung San, "Burma's Challenge," in Josef Silverstein, ed., *Aung San's Political Legacy* (Ithica, New York: Cornell University, 1972), p. 40.
Chapter Five
A Quiet Young Woman

[14] Mya Maung, *Totalitarianism in Burma: Prospects for Economic Development* (New York: Paragon House, 1992), p. 140.

[15] The *New York Times*, 15 October 1991.

[16] Aung San Suu Kyi, "The Need for Solidarity among Ethnic Groups," in Michael Aris, ed., *Freedom From Fear* (New York: Penguin, 1991), pp. 227-8.

[17] Aung San Suu Kyi, in *The New York Times*, 21 July 1989.
Chapter Six
Scholar, Wife And Mother

[18] All the following Ann Slater quotes from Ann Pasternak Slater, "Suu Burmese," in *Freedom From Fear*, pp. 258-266 *passim*.

[19] Current Biography Yearbook, p. 28.

[20] Aung San Suu Kyi, "In the Eye of the Revolution," in *Freedom From Fear*, p. 212.

[21] Aung San Suu Kyi, in The *New York Times*, 11 January, 1989.

[22] Slater, "Suu Burmese," pp. 262, 264.

Chapter Seven
Unrest In Burma Begins

[23] Aung San Suu Kyi, "In the Eye of the Revolution," in *Freedom From Fear*, p. 212.

[24] Lintner, *Outrage: Burma's Struggle for Democracy* (London: White Lotus, 1990), p.95.

Chapter Eight
Fated For Politics

[25] Aung San Suu Kyi, "The First Initiative," *Freedom From Fear*, p. 193.

[26] *Ibid.*

[27] *Ibid.*, p. 195.

[28] This and all subsequent quotations from Aung San Suu Kyi's Shwedagon speech are from Aung San Suu Kyi, "Speech at the Shwedagon Pagoda," in *Freedom From Fear*, pp. 198-204.

[29] Aung San Suu Kyi, "The Objectives" in *Freedom From Fear*, pp. 205-6.

[30] Aung San Suu Kyi, "The Objectives" in *Freedom From Fear*, pp. 206-7.

[31] The *New York Times*, 11 January 1989.

[32] Mya Maung, pp. 147-8.

[33] Lintner, *Outrage*, p. 133.

[34] The *Times* (London), 3 January 1989.

[35] The *Far Eastern Economic Review*, 11 May 1989.
Chapter Nine
Under Arrest

[36] The *New York Times*, 16 August 1990.

[37] Aung San Suu Kyi, speech to the International Human
Rights Law Group, delivered by Alexander Aris, 14 May
1992.

[38] Aung San Suu Kyi, "Freedom From Fear," in *Freedom
From Fear*, pp. 180-1.

[39] *Ibid.*, p.184.
Chapter Ten
A Resolution Without An End

[40] Aung San Suu Kyi, "The Need for Solidarity among
Ethnic Groups," in *Freedom From Fear*, p. 230.

INDEX